T0316697

Cambridge Elements ≡

Elements in Shakespeare and Text
edited by
Claire M. L. Bourne
The Pennsylvania State University
Rory Loughnane
University of Kent

EDITING ARCHIPELAGIC SHAKESPEARE

Rory Loughnane
University of Kent

Willy Maley
University of Glasgow

CAMBRIDGE
UNIVERSITY PRESS

CAMBRIDGE
UNIVERSITY PRESS

Shaftesbury Road, Cambridge CB2 8EA, United Kingdom

One Liberty Plaza, 20th Floor, New York, NY 10006, USA

477 Williamstown Road, Port Melbourne, VIC 3207, Australia

314–321, 3rd Floor, Plot 3, Splendor Forum, Jasola District Centre,
New Delhi – 110025, India

103 Penang Road, #05–06/07, Visioncrest Commercial, Singapore 238467

Cambridge University Press is part of Cambridge University Press & Assessment,
a department of the University of Cambridge.

We share the University's mission to contribute to society through the pursuit of
education, learning and research at the highest international levels of excellence.

www.cambridge.org
Information on this title: www.cambridge.org/9781009521949

DOI: 10.1017/9781009521925

© Rory Loughnane and Willy Maley 2024

First published 2024

A catalogue record for this publication is available from the British Library

ISBN 978-1-009-52194-9 Paperback
ISSN 2754-4257 (online)
ISSN 2754-4249 (print)

Additional resources for this publication at www.cambridge.org/Loughnane

Editing Archipelagic Shakespeare

Elements in Shakespeare and Text

DOI: 10.1017/9781009521925
First published online: November 2024

Rory Loughnane
University of Kent

Willy Maley
University of Glasgow

Author for correspondence: Rory Loughnane, R.Loughnane@kent.ac.uk

ABSTRACT: *Editing Archipelagic Shakespeare* is a study of the power of names; more specifically, it is about the power of naming, asking who gets to choose names, for what reason, and to what effect. Shakespeare assigns names to over 1,200 characters and countless more sites and places, and these names, or versions of these names, have become familiar to generations of playgoers and play-readers. And because of their familiarity, Shakespeare's names, most frequently anglicized versions of non-English names, have been accepted and repeated without further consideration. Approaching names from an archipelagic perspective, and focusing upon how Irish, Scottish, and Welsh characters and places are written by Shakespeare and treated by editors, this Element offers an expansive, and far-reaching, case study for non-anglophone and global studies of Shakespeare, textual scholarship, and early modern drama.

This Element also has a video abstract: Cambridge.org/ESTX_Loughnane

KEYWORDS: character names, textual editing, editorial practice, national identities, editorial tradition

ISBNs: 9781009521949 (PB), 9781009521925 (OC)
ISSNs: 2754-4257 (online), 2754-4249 (print)

Contents

Introduction: Archipelagic Shakespeare and the Editing of Names

In his prologue to our edited collection, *Celtic Shakespeare*, John Kerrigan asked: 'Is it not better described ... as *archipelagic* Shakespeare?'[1] In what follows, we map out the contours of archipelagic Shakespeare and ask what this might mean not only for criticism but for editing early modern dramatic writing. In a recent essay, Judy Celine Ick approaches this topic from another angle: 'This new map that looks at 'Archipelagic Shakespeare' presents a challenge to the maps of 'Global Shakespeare'. ... a shift to an archipelagic imagination [that] allows us to see the different 'islands' – performances, translations, adaptations, and other incarnations scattered across the globe – as intricately related and these relationships as constitutive of Shakespeare itself'.[2]

Working at the intersection of historical and textual scholarship, our aim in this study is to home in on the Atlantic Archipelago, and to explore how English and non-English characters from this region are identified, named, and characterized in Shakespeare's plays. Our approach is to situate Shakespeare's writing of these characters in the context of his and others' intercultural interactions in late Elizabethan

---

[1] John Kerrigan, 'Prologue: *Díonbrollach*: How Celtic Was Shakespeare?', in Willy Maley and Rory Loughnane, eds., *Celtic Shakespeare: The Bard and the Borderers* (Farnham, Surrey: Ashgate, 2013), pp. xv–xli, at p. xxiii; emphasis in original. Kerrigan trailed the concept in 'Archipelagic *Macbeth*', in *Archipelagic English: Literature, History, and Politics 1603–1707* (Oxford: Oxford University Press, 2008), pp. 91–114. We anticipated the shift from Celtic concerns to archipelagic matters in setting the scene for our collection: 'Introduction: Celtic Connections and Archipelagic Angles', in Loughnane and Maley, eds., *Celtic Shakespeare*, pp. 1–22.

[2] Judy Celine Ick, 'The Augmentation of the Indies: An Archipelagic Approach to Asian and Global Shakespeare', in Bi-qi Beatrice Lei, Judy Celine Ick and Poonam Trivedi, eds., *Shakespeare's Asian Journeys: Critical Encounters, Cultural Geographies, and the Politics of Travel* (London: Routledge, 2017), p. 33 (pp. 19–36).

and early Jacobean London. We are especially interested in how Shakespeare named his non-English archipelagic characters, in how these names were spelled, and in why Shakespeare might have decided upon these names. But we also wish to use the example of the archipelago to think more globally – historically, geographically, and linguistically – about how, when, and why certain names and spellings became adopted in Shakespeare's texts, in his day and throughout the historical editorial tradition, and the editorial and critical concomitants that arise from naming practices.

Names are powerful signifiers that push beyond simply distinguishing one person or character from another.[3] As an author immersed in theatrical practice, Shakespeare would have been acutely aware of how character names can matter in both a dramatic and practical sense. In a pun-laden theatrical and broader culture, names were not chosen randomly or haphazardly. While largely eschewing the bluntly allegorical or pun-rich names familiar to readers of Jonson (e.g., Volpone, Sir Epicure Mammon) and Middleton (e.g., Vindice, Whorehound), Shakespeare frequently deployed or adapted names to pointed effect: think of the diminutive familiar form of 'Hal' given to 'Prince Henry' in his raucous early days. As Shakespeare knew well, names can and do affect how audiences and readers understand characters.

We are now some 400 years from when Shakespeare's first editions introduced and solidified certain forms of names for certain characters. We insist upon 'forms of names' because, of course, spelling varied greatly in the period and a chosen name could appear in manuscript and print in various iterations. Such variation in spelling could originate at any part of the (not necessarily linear) process from the autograph manuscript to the various playhouse documents to the printshop.[4] As the great majority of

---

[3] Laurie Maguire's *Shakespeare's Names* (Oxford: Oxford University Press, 2007) offers a series of excellent case studies.

[4] Recent work on the mediation of Shakespeare's scripts includes the essays in Roslyn L. Knutson, David McInnis and Matthew Steggle, eds., *Loss and the Literary Culture of Shakespeare's Time* (Basingstoke: Palgrave Macmillan, 2020).

Shakespeare's plays were drawn from earlier printed source materials, he frequently adopted forms of names found in the sources consulted. Still, this process was not entirely straightforward, and Shakespeare altered names as he saw fit. Writing for a group of (largely) English actors acting for (largely) English audiences, Shakespeare introduced forms of names, especially for non-English characters, that could be easily read and easily pronounced. There was, it seems, little point in retaining a name's form from the source if it would distract or confuse the intended reader (the actor) and listener (the audience member).[5] Shakespeare was, in effect, his own first editor, producing anglicized, fairly regularized forms of non-Anglophone names to make them intelligible for actors and audiences.

Thus, in Q1 *1 Henry IV* (1598) readers encounter variants of 'Owen Glendower' (including 'Glondower'), an anglicized form of the (modern) Welsh 'Owain Glyn Dŵr'. The spelling of this name was not regularized in Welsh in the early modern period – no names were, and spellings were largely unfixed – and Shakespeare approximated a blunt yet still recognizable version of the Welsh name. Similarly, consider the case of Shakespeare's most famous character. Why is 'Hamlet' named 'Hamlet'? Why not 'Amleth', as per Shakespeare's primary source, Francois Belleforest's *Histoire Tragiques*? Or the Latinized 'Amlethus', as per Belleforest's source, Saxo Grammaticus' *Gesta Danorum*? Or the old Irish form 'Admlithi' from the story *Togail Bruidne Da Derga*, which could have been transmitted to Saxo?[6] The easy answer is that 'Hamlet' is named 'Hamlet' in *Hamlet* because Shakespeare gave him this name and that is how it appears in the early printed version(s) of this play. But how did Shakespeare arrive at the name 'Hamlet'?[7] Is 'Hamlet' simply Shakespeare's

---

[5] It is plausible that certain names and forms were road-tested by actors in rehearsal. For practices in rehearsal, see Tiffany Stern, *Rehearsal from Shakespeare to Sheridan* (Oxford: Oxford University Press, 2007), *passim*.

[6] Lisa A. Collinson, 'A New Etymology for *Hamlet*? The names *Amlethus, Amlođi* and *Admlithi*', *Review of English Studies* 62, 257 (2011): 675–694.

[7] Searching through the EEBO-TCP database, the word 'Hamlet' appears in sixty-five works printed before 1603, when Q1 of *Hamlet* was first published. In sixty-three of these works, many with multiple hits for the word, 'hamlet' means, as it still does, small settlement or village. A contemporary dictionary glosses the word

anglicized version of 'Amleth'? Did 'Hamlet' *sound* sufficiently Danish? Was Shakespeare thinking practically that 'Hamlet' was an easier pronunciation for actors than 'Amleth'? Or for audiences? Or was Shakespeare thinking personally, and found something resonant in the verbal proximity of the names 'Hamlet' and 'Hamnet', his son (*d.* 1596), named after a Stratford neighbour? The key point here is that names included in early modern stage plays represent a choice, most often made by the dramatist. And this choice invariably veers towards an anglicized version of non-Anglophone names found in source materials.

Another choice, made much later, is how names found in the early modern manuscript or printed text are presented to readers in regularized, modernized formats in editions. No editor in the history of Shakespearean scholarship has dared, or would care to dare, to change 'Hamlet' to 'Amleth' or the other options. But is the retention of 'Hamlet' a case of staying true to the original author's intentions (a risky assumption, always) and to the spelling of the originally printed text(s), or a perpetuation of an Anglo-centric practice, instituted by Shakespeare, of renaming non-Anglophone words for English consumption? Or is 'Hamlet' just 'Hamlet', consolidated by a historical literary-critical tradition? This study asks, in turn, what governs, and has governed, editorial decision-making about names and naming and what implications it might have for criticism and performance?

In recent years, there has been much discussion about efforts to de-canonize, and thereby decolonize, teaching curricula and research canons. In this study, we will show how it is not simply the plays themselves but how they are edited for, and presented to a modern-day readership, that helps ingrain culturally attenuated historical readings of non-English identities.

"*Hamelet*. Cut off, abated". See J. B., *An English Expositor: Teaching the Interpretation of the Hardest Words vsed in Our Language. With Sundry Explications, Descriptions, and Discourses* (London: 1621), A4[r]. The other two works, Thomas Lodge's *Wit's Misery* (1596) and Thomas Dekker's *Satiromastix* (1602) refer, indisputably, to the stage character. For Q1 *Hamlet* representing an early version of Shakespeare's play, see Terri Bourus, *Young Shakespeare's Young Hamlet: Print, Piracy, and Performance* (New York: Palgrave Macmillan, 2014).

This study examines how Shakespeare names characters and places from outside England in the Atlantic Archipelago – in Ireland, Scotland, and Wales. One exemplary passage – the Four Captains scene in *Henry V* 3.3 – works as a testing ground for archipelagic editorial work, as well as a crucible for critical revaluation, pedagogical practice, and performance. The scene brings together on a battlefield in France four officers from England, Ireland, Scotland, and Wales, ostensibly fighting for the English crown, but also fighting among themselves. On one view, '*Henry V* is a hybrid play united and divided primarily between textual historiography and dramatic performance'.[8] Early studies recognized the significance of this episode where Shakespeare 'brings on the stage at the same time representatives of all three Celtic peoples – Macmorris, Fluellin, and Captain Jamy'.[9] This early twentieth-century scholarship was never incorporated into editorial practice, which remained irresolutely Anglocentric. More recent work has also failed to alter the trajectory of editorial practice. We are struck by the fact that two recurrent waves of archipelagic scholarship have failed to impact significantly on textual scholarship in early modern studies, even despite some excellent archipelagic editors (including Irish critics like Edward Dowden and Scots-born or based scholars such as A. C. Bradley, John Dover Wilson, and Peter Alexander, not to mention the Dublin-born Edmond Malone, Shakespeare's greatest editor of the late eighteenth century).

'A climax of absurdity' is how A. L. Morton described the archipelagic scene in *Henry V*, and he sees perception of unity as a persistent anachronism: 'The implication of a "British" nation is not only absurd for the fifteenth century but almost equally so for Shakespeare's own time, while even today the national position of Wales and Scotland is still a controversial matter and no one would deny that Ireland has always been a totally distinct nation'.[10] The

---

[8] Clifford Stetner, 'Colonizing Ireland in the Hybrid Performance/Text of Shakespeare's *Henry V*', *LATCH* 2 (2009): 18 (17–53).

[9] Edward D. Snyder, 'The Wild Irish: A Study of Some English Satires against the Irish, Scots, and Welsh', *Modern Philology* 17, 12 (1920): 703 (687–725).

[10] A. L. Morton, *The Matter of Britain: Essays in a Living Culture* (London: Lawrence & Wishart, 1966), p. 47.

last part of this statement is up for debate, not least of all in Shakespeare's play. More Anglocentrically, Jonathan Baldo asserted that: 'The four captains ... bear testimony to the Elizabethans' growing conviction that the national unit was not England but England, Wales, Scotland, and Ireland'.[11] But this scene was only first printed in Jacobean England, in what has been called the century of the three kingdoms.

In focusing upon an exemplary archipelagic scene, and its editing, we are excavating an archipelagic moment that was shut down within decades. We pick up the scent with the phrase 'I smell the bloud of an English-man', clearly a commonplace by 1596, when it is used by Thomas Nashe in his takedown of Gabriel Harvey's scholarly pretensions: 'O tis a precious apothegmaticall Pedant, who will finde matter inough to dilate a whole daye of the first inuention of *Fy, fa, fum*, I smell the bloud of an English-man'.[12] This bogeyman rhyme has as an archipelagic echo in the wake of the Union of Crowns in Edgar's 'I smell the bloud of a British man' in *King Lear* (Q1, G3^r). Shakespeare was an archipelagic editor. Conversely, the Steward's allusion to 'The *British* partie' in Q1 (20.230) becomes 'the English party' in the Folio.[13] Is the Quarto more archipelagic?

What Nashe says of Harvey, Matthew Arnold thought of John Ruskin's onomatomania:

> I will not say that the meaning of Shakespeare's names (I put aside the question as to the correctness of Ruskin's etymologies) has no effect at all, may be entirely lost sight of; but to give it that degree of prominence is to throw the reins to one's whim, to forget all moderation and proportion, to lose the

---

[11] Jonathan Baldo, 'Wars of Memory in *Henry V*', *Shakespeare Quarterly* 47, 2 (1996): 146 (132–159).

[12] Thomas Nashe, *Haue with You to Saffron-walden* (London: 1596), F3^r.

[13] *M. William Shakespeare HIS True Chronicle Historie of the life and death of King LEAR* (London: [Nicholas Okes] for Nathaniel Butter, 1608). All citations to Shakespeare's works, unless otherwise stated, are from the original spelling editions in the *New Oxford Shakespeare: Critical Reference Edition*, 2 Vols. (Oxford: Oxford University Press, 2017).

balance of one's mind altogether. It is to show in one's criticism, to the highest excess, the note of provinciality.[14]

We may run the risk of being the Harvey and Ruskin of Shakespeare studies, but we believe that Shakespeare's names matter. Names were a touchy subject in the period, and surnames more so, hovering somewhere between family name, placename, and nickname.[15] In *Lucrece* we have 'Lvcius Tarquinius (*for his excessive pride surnamed* Superbus)' (Argvement. 1); in *Titus Andronicus* the new emperor is '*Andronicus,* surnamed *Pius*:/ For many good and great deserts to Rome' (1.23–4); and Caius Martius draws attention to his surname by noting that 'The extreme Dangers, and the droppes of Blood/ Shed for my thanklesse country are requitted/ But with that Surname'. (*Coriolanus*, 4.5.64–66). In Ireland names were an especially hot topic. The post-Reformation process of 'surrender and regrant' saw Irish lords relinquish native titles for English earldoms, so that 'the name of O'Neill', for example, was forbidden and its owner expected to assume the new title of earl of Tyrone. The name is conjured up in moments of crisis, as in Marlowe's *Edward II*:

> The wilde *Oneyle*, with swarmes of Irish Kernes,
> Liues vncontroulde within the English pale.[16]

After the Nine Years War the 2nd earl, Hugh O'Neil, renounced 'the name and title of O'Neill'.[17] Names retained an incantatory power long after the deaths of the individuals associated with them.

While our focus here will be exclusively upon the Atlantic Archipelago, the broader aims and findings of the study extend far beyond this region.

---

[14] Matthew Arnold, 'The Literary Influence of Academies', *The Cornhill Magazine* 10 (1864): 168 (154–172). See Richard Coates, 'A Provincial Bibliography on Names in the Works of Shakespeare', *Names* 35, 3–4 (1987): 206–223.

[15] Patrick Gordon, *The famous historie of the renouned and valiant Prince Robert surnamed the Bruce King of Scotland* (Dort: 1615).

[16] Christopher Marlowe, *The Troublesome Raigne and Lamentable Death of Edward the Second* (London: 1594), E1ᵛ.

[17] G. A. Hayes-McCoy, 'The Making of an O'Neill: A View of the Ceremony at Tullaghoge, Co. Tyrone', *Ulster Journal of Archaeology* 33 (1970): 89 (89–94).

Editing Archipelagic Shakespeare means editing Shakespeare 'archipelagically', that is, in light of archipelagic studies like John Kerrigan's that remind us of the diverse and multiple nature of the nations and polities at play in the period, and which Shakespeare's work encompasses, specifically for our purposes the Celtic nations of Ireland, Scotland, and Wales. But it also means editing 'Archipelagic Shakespeare', since Shakespeare is always already archipelagic, before being reshaped over four centuries by an Anglocentric editorial and critical tradition. In this sense when we are editing 'Archipelagic Shakespeare' we are 'Unediting Anglocentric Shakespeare'. Our analysis of the Four Captains, their names, their naming, and the perpetuation of their names in the critical and editorial traditions, will, we hope, direct new attention, to the extraordinary but unexamined implications of practices of anglicization, regularization, and modernization. But before we get to the names of the Four Captains, let us first consider how the names found in Shakespeare's plays came to be fixed entities.

1 Editing Names

In Nicholas Rowe's dedication to the Duke of Somerset in the first volume of his 1709 edition, Shakespeare's first editor writes:

> I have sometimes had the Honour to hear Your Grace express the particular Pleasure you have taken in that Greatness of Thought, those natural Images, those Passions finely touch'd, and that beautiful Expression which is every where to be met in *Shakespear*. And that he may still have the Honour to entertain Your Grace, I have taken some Care to redeem him of the Injuries of former Impressions. I must not pretend to have restor'd this Work to the Exactness of the Author's Original Manuscripts: Those are lost, or, at least, are gone beyond any Inquiry I could make; so that there was nothing left, but to compare the several Editions, and give the true Reading as well as I could from thence. This I have endeavour'd to do pretty

carefully, and render'd very many Places Intelligible, that
were not so before. (A2^{r-v})

The editorial toil Rowe describes – identifying printshop errors ('redeem-
[ing] him of the Injuries of former Impressions'), collation work ('compar-
[ing] the several editions'), and introducing emendations for meaning
('render'd very many Places Intelligible') – will be recognizable to all
those who have used a modern critical edition or edited an early modern
play. Rowe here sets out a job description for editorial work which retains
currency today. Yet Rowe omits other crucial parts of his labour: the
regularization of Shakespeare's plays.[18] Across six volumes, Rowe introduces the following regular forms for each play: character lists, or '*dramatis
personae*', ordered by social rank (top to bottom) and gender (male characters before female); act and scene breaks; stage directions that are centred
for entrances and aligned right for exits (other stage directions are also
largely aligned right); and, developing from his character lists, non-variant
speech prefixes for each character.[19] Rowe's editorial project, and his
innovations with producing a regularized edition, were apiece with
a larger vernacular editorial project initiated by Rowe's publisher, Jacob
Tonson.[20] The regularization of the features of the Shakespearean texts

[18] Rowe's *Works* did not include Shakespeare's poetry.

[19] As Andrew Murphy notes, Rowe also 'increased the number of indicators of
location included in the text, in some cases taking his cue from Restoration
adaptations of the plays'. Andrew Murphy, *Shakespeare in Print* (Cambridge and
New York: Cambridge University Press, 2003), p. 61.

[20] As Robert B. Hamm notes, 'Over the course of a decade, the house refined this
style and used it to print a number of authors, including those – such as
Shakespeare – whose collections had been out of print for some time. Authors
in the vernacular series include: Beaumont and Fletcher (1712), Congreve (1710,
1719), Cowley (1707, 1710), Denham (1709), Dryden (1717), Etherege (1715),
Jonson (1716), Milton (1711, 1720), Otway (1712), Shadwell (1720), Shakespeare
(1709,1714), Spenser (1715), Suckling (1709), Vanbrugh (1719), and Waller
(1711)'. See Robert B. Hamm, "Rowe's "Shakespear" (1709) and the Tonson
House Style", *College Literature* 31, no. 3 (2004): 179–205.

helped eighteenth-century readers navigate their way through the works: if they could read one Shakespeare play, they could read them all.

Rowe's edition established certain protocols and procedures for producing editions of early modern drama. His edition also helped establish the use of certain character names, as well as regularized abbreviated speech prefixes for character names. These often five letters in length at a maximum, but typically four letters: thus, '*Bene*' and '*Beat*' in *Much Ado*, but also '*Pedro*'. Full character names were given in stage directions (in roman type unlike the rest of the italicized stage direction), although the designation tended to follow his copy text rather than selected speech prefix, therefore creating some potential confusion in reading. Most significantly, Rowe's character lists revealed his choice of spelling, while his speech prefixes revealed his favoured character designation. Even so, he was not always consistent; for example, the Irish Captain is identified as '*Mackmorris*' in his list of characters, as 'Mackmorrice' in stage directions and dialogue, and as the more ambiguous '*Mack*' in speech prefixes. We dwell on Rowe's edition, and some of his choices, simply to note that as the editorial tradition for Shakespeare's plays began in earnest, so too certain forms and spellings of character names came to be instituted within that tradition that continue into modern day.

As modern readers of Shakespeare we learn to have certain expectations, and these have been conditioned by the regularizing practices of Rowe and his inheritors. The Shakespeare most people first encounter, in the form of a modern-spelling edition, is designed to bring him closer to us as modern readers, rather than us to him, an early modern poet and dramatist. Though editions may vary in some respects, most modern-spelling editions adhere to the same understood conventions, only some of which are inherited from the earliest printed texts as opposed to the subsequent editorial tradition: an introduction, written by the editor or another scholar; a list of characters; a modernized text; distinct verse and prose lineation arrangements; glossarial notes coded to the text; act and scene numbering; marginal line numbering; italicized stage directions; and regularized speech prefixes to indicate which character is speaking. If you are reading a scholarly edition, you can also expect to find textual notes and lineation notes, each with some form of collation of variant readings drawn from early printed texts and influential editions.[21] Such editorial apparatuses are included to ease the reader's entry into the text. But these apparatuses also function to assure the reader that the Shakespeare play they are reading can be trusted; that it has been carefully prepared. Freed from the burden of working through a copy or facsimile of an original-spelling early modern printed text, with its errors and inconsistencies of spelling and format, readers can more easily focus on the 'literary' work at hand.

Readers of Shakespeare may assume then that any errors or inconsistencies are 'emended' or 'resolved' in an even-handed way by editors. After all, much editorial decision-making belongs within a long and respected tradition. There, in fact, lies a serious problem. While it is true that editions tend to evolve and there are accretions as well as interjections of fresh critical perspectives, the great expanse of past Shakespearean editions produces its own set of restraints for editors. An entirely new textual emendation or reading is, in this sense, always radical, pushing back against the weight of tradition. As a result, editors often tend towards the conservative, the received, the accepted. And, in this way, certain readings, once newly introduced, are repeated verbatim or only lightly modified from earliest editions to later, sometimes without comment as they are consumed into tradition. The editorial tradition helps to canonize many readings, leaving those first altered readings unchallenged. The Shakespeare editor, like the reader, is then unburdened by the past process of unburdening.

Of editorial tasks, as Rowe makes clear, emendations are the headline act. Practices of regularization and modernization, though often significantly more laborious than emending a word, phrase, or line, typically lurk somewhere offstage. One editorial output that combines regularization with modernization passes almost entirely without notice: speech prefixes.[22] Hiding in plain sight, speech prefixes in modern editions are often offset to the left of the dialogue and

---

[21] See Marcus Walsh, *Shakespeare*, *Milton and Eighteenth-Century Literary Editing* (Cambridge: Cambridge University Press, 1997), and Murphy, *Shakespeare in Print*.

[22] There has only been one book-length study of speech prefixes to our knowledge: A collection of essays edited by George Walton Williams, ed., *Shakespeare's Speech-Headings: Speaking the Speech in Shakespeare's Plays* (Cranbury: University of Delaware Press, 1997). See also R. B. McKerrow's essay in *The Review of English Studies* XI, 44 (1935): 459–465.

typographically distinguished in some way (e.g., emboldened, italicized, and small capital letters). In other cases, they are part of the same unit of text, set off with an indent.[23] They are at once functional and formulaic – indicating to the reader that Character A is speaking rather than Character B or C and doing so in a consistent way. They are also formal – a speech prefix indicates that the dialogue positioned thereafter is to be spoken aloud by that specific individual character[24]; they indicate that what someone is reading is drama and not a poem, a novel, or a short story or some other literary form. The reader, encountering a speech prefix first in their sequential reading of a text, must assign what is subsequently spoken to a character distinct from the previous or next speaker. The editorial practice with speech prefixes primarily seeks, therefore, to eliminate doubt for the reader about which character is speaking. Once uncertainty is removed, excavated by editors, the reader is free to more closely examine what characters say than how those characters are identified. It has been this way ever since Rowe's edition in 1709. Over 300 years of adopting this practice has helped create an expectation for this functional, formulaic, and formal feature.

But, while speech prefixes in early printed texts of Shakespeare may be similarly functional and formal, they are not always formulaic. Variation in character names can reflect, sometimes problematically or reductively, that the character has both a personal name and a role (e.g., Feste as variations of '*Clown*' throughout *Twelfth Night*, indicating his role in Olivia's household). There are examples in Shakespeare's plays when the alignment of speech prefix and circumstance seems so specific, however, that it merits further analysis. The variant speech prefixes assigned to Bertram's mother in *All's Well that Ends Well*, for example, often seem situational: when she is around Bertram, she might be '*Mother*'; '*Lady*', when in the company of servants; '*Old Lady*', when around the younger Helen; and '*Countess*' when at the court on official business. Or consider, the one usage of '*Harry*' in *2 Henry IV* which occurs when the Prince and his father are left alone onstage,

---

[23] See Claire M. L. Bourne, *Typographies of Performance in Early Modern England* (Oxford: Oxford University Press, 2020), Chapter 1.

[24] There are exceptions. Some speech prefixes, for example, designate multiple speakers (e.g., '*Omnes.*').

as Henry, carrying the crown, plaintively says 'I never thought to hear you speak again' (4.3.221). What follows, as the King wonders if Harry wishes him already dead so that he can succeed to the throne, is an intergenerational struggle, familiar in essence to many father–son relationships, that is less about monarchical control and more about what it means to take on greater responsibility as one ages. Does the sudden outcropping of the familiar '*Harry*' better support this dynamic than the heretofore used formal title of '*Prince*', or is it simply a coincidence? With both examples, when editors opt to introduce the regularized modern-speech prefix, typically '*Countess*' and '*Prince*' for these characters, does it diminish the reading experience of specific moments in these plays in a meaningful way?

Given the variation in early printed play texts, on what principle might an editor favour one name over another? Whatever decision they make will feed into their character lists, stage directions, and speech prefixes, so it should not be taken lightly. Should an editor, for instance, always opt for the name *first used* in a stage direction? Or *first used* in a speech prefix? The first time the usurping brother speaks in Q2 *Hamlet*, he is designated as '*Claud.*', an abbreviation of his first name, 'Claudius', as introduced in the opening stage direction to the play's second scene. This seems a solid choice, then, for an editor producing a regularized modern-spelling edition of that text. But this would be to ignore that the subsequent 107 speech prefixes for this character each read a version of '*King*'. Should editors, then, always resort to the *most-often used* name? If so, an editor would opt for '*Shylock*' (versions of which are used in speech prefixes fifty-three times) over '*Jew*' (twenty-six times in speech prefixes) for Antonio's antagonist.[25]

---

[25] John Drakakis proposed in his Arden 3 edition of *The Merchant of Venice* that 'Shylock was designated throughout the manuscript by the speech prefix "Jew"', supposing that an exhaustion of italic and Roman capital '*I*' forced the compositor to switch to the proper name. (See John Drakakis, ed. *The Merchant of Venice*, Arden Third Series (London: The Arden Shakespeare, 2010), p. 422; the argument itself was extrapolated from Richard F. Kennedy, 'Speech Prefixes in Some Shakespearean Quartos', *PBSA* 92 (1998), 177–209). Gabriel Egan demonstrated the implausibility of this justification for the variant Shylock/Jew usage in this instance. See 'Shakespeare: Editions and Textual Matters' in William Baker and

But is it not curious that nineteen of those versions of the speech prefix '*Jew*' occur in the trial scene of 4.1 (the first ten of which use only this designator)? In abiding by a *most-often used* principle, and thereby rejecting the ethno-religious designator of '*Jew*', might the editorial act of unburdening the reader be better characterized as unenlightening?

And what if the deployment of a *single* speech prefix based on either the *first-used* or *most-often used* principle is impossible or seems absurd? In Q1 *2 Henry IV* (1600), the speech prefix switches from '*Prince*' or '*Harry*' to '*King*' after the coronation (and, notably, the rejection of Falstaff). This makes good narrative sense, but it produces a real difficulty for editors: there are two English kings named Henry in the play.[26] An editor could opt for using simply '*Harry*' throughout, avoiding the problem raised with a change in titles. But this would mean opting for a speech prefix that is used just once in Q1 (at 13.221), and one that is problematic in terms of comparison with Prince John, Harry's brother, who is designated variously as versions of '*John*', '*Prince*', '*Lancaster*', and '*Brother*', but primarily as '*Prince*'. So, an editor might end up sticking to their *most-often used* guns and use '*Prince*' for Hal, as Line Cottegnies does in the 2016 Norton Third Edition. But this creates the anomalous situation whereby we have two brothers, one named PRINCE and the other PRINCE JOHN, until the play's final scene proper (scene 18; 5.5 in the Norton) where the former changes designation to KING, in a play where we have already had a KING character, who is now dead (long live the KING).[27] Or consider the final scene proper of *Henry*

Kenneth Womack, eds., *The Year's Work in English Studies*. Vol. 91, (Oxford: Oxford University Press, 2012), pp. 337–342. Type exhaustion is however a plausible explanation in some cases of varied usage: See Peter W. M. Blayney's argument about pressure on capital italic 'E' with the names of Edmund and Edward in Q1 *King Lear* in *The texts of* King Lear *and Their Origins*, Vol 1 (Cambridge: Cambridge University Press, 1982), pp. 129–130. For another example of such compositor practices, see John Jowett, 'Ligature Shortage and Speech-prefix Variation in Julius Caesar' *The Library* 6,3 (1984): 244–253.

[26] This is a difficulty that would be immediately evident to any modern editors using TEI-XML which relies upon singular markers and cannot tolerate ambiguity.

[27] And this is even though he is already King during his appearance in Scene 15 (where he is still described as '*the prince*' by Warwick (15.42)). Francis X.

V (5.2) when during the marriage negotiations Henry alternates between '*England*' and '*King*' while encountering '*France*' (meaning the King of France; one time '*French King*' is used), '*Quee*' (meaning the French Queen, Isabel), and '*Kath*' (for Katherine, the only personal name used). In such a scene, would the power play involved in the negotiations be undersold by regularizing on some principle?

Where variation in character names exists, editorial decision-making exists. Yet the names preferred and chosen, particularly in Shakespeare, can feel crushed under the weight of editorial tradition. Certain forms of character names have become ingrained in the Shakespearean editorial tradition with little consideration about the how or why of the forms selected. Editors, in selecting and implementing regularized character names, are often faced with not only a textual quandary but also a critical, if not political, one. And we should recall that in implementing regularized character names, editors must delete those varied forms they are rejecting.[28] This process of deletion, based on an editorial decision to favour one designator over another, is rendered invisible to the reader. Some editorial series such as the Arden 3 include a set of prefatory notes following the 'List of Roles' in which the editor(s) delineate the character names. Here, for example, is Jonathan Bate's note about an important character in *Titus Andronicus*:

> AARON 'Aron' in Qq (and Ravenscroft), but eds since
> Rowe follow F's Aaron. The pun on 'air' at 4.2.17 l supports
> this spelling in terms of pronunciation. An Elizabeth audi-
> ence would have known that the biblical Aaron had an

Connor, in his edition for the *New Oxford Shakespeare: Modern Critical Edition* (Oxford: Oxford University Press, 2016), opted to deploy PRINCE HARRY until this scene where he modified an entrance stage direction to read '*Enter the Prince [as King] . . .*' and thereafter uses the speech prefix KING HARRY.

[28] On the negative textual interference of modern editors, see, for example, Randall McLeod, 'Un 'Editing' Shak-Speare', *SubStance* 10/11 (1981): 26–55; Margreta de Grazia and Peter Stallybrass. 'The Materiality of the Shakespearean Text', *Shakespeare Quarterly* 44, no. 3 (1993): 255–283; and Leah Marcus, *Unediting the Renaissance: Shakespeare, Marlowe Milton* (London and New York: Routledge, 1996).

eloquent, persuasive tongue (Exodus, 4.10–16). 'Aron' was
a bitter plant, *serpentia minor*, which is also apt.[29]

The information on punning and the name's biblical and horticultural associations is useful but let us focus on that first sentence which covers a lot of
ground.[30] Bate notes that 'Aron' is used in the quarto printings while the
spelling shifts to 'Aaron' in the First Folio. This is, strictly speaking, only true
in that 'Aaron' is used in dialogue and stage directions but '*Aron.*' is used
repeatedly in most Folio speech prefixes. He then notes the longstanding
editorial tradition, since Rowe no less, of using the form 'Aaron'. Such
a minor bone of contention over the spelling/pronunciation of 'A(a)ron'
rather buries the lede concerning this character's name: in both Qq and F,
there is alteration in speech prefixes between a designation of the character's
proper name and a form of 'M(o)or(e)'.[31] In Q1, for example, following the
long opening scene '*manet Moore*' (i.e., he remains onstage), and then the
character is assigned the speech prefix '*Aron*' given for the subsequent speech.
But after Chiron and Demetrius enter to him, the speech prefix changes to
'*Moore*' for his next four speeches. Then, Chiron says '*Aron*', A thousand
deaths would I propose/ To atchiue her whom I loue' and the speech prefix
alternates to '*Aron*' for that speech before reverting again to '*Moore*' for the
next three speeches, reverting to '*Aron*' again for the final speech.[32] As it is

---

[29] Jonathan Bate, ed. *Titus Andronicus*, revised edition, The Arden Shakespeare
(London and New York: Bloomsbury, 2018), p. 165.

[30] The reference to 'Qq' means the three early quartos of the play (1594, 1600,
1611).

[31] A more remarkable (and lastingly influential) spelling-based error is the case of
'Imogen', used repeatedly in the First Folio text of *Cymbeline*, but almost
certainly a minim error ('nn' read as 'm') for 'Innogen', the name used consis-
tently in Shakespeare's sources. See Rory Loughnane, ed. *Cymbeline* in the *New
Oxford Shakespeare: Critical Reference Edition*, Vol. 2 (Oxford: Oxford
University Press, 2017), p. 3356. For a contrasting view in defence of
'Imogen', see Ros King, *Cymbeline: Constructions of Britain* (Aldershot and
Burlington: Ashgate, 2005), p. 72.

[32] This is a passage most likely written by George Peele, but such variation also
extends into the Shakespearean parts of the play. On the play's co-authorship, see

unlikely such potentially confusing variation would have been introduced by a compositor (the person or persons setting type in the printshop), we must suspect that it reflects the manuscript underlying the quarto text. We might, for example, explain the switch to '*Aron*' following Chiron's speech because the author had just used the proper name and it was in their mind as they wrote the next speech prefix. But the more important point is that the character's proper name and the ethnographic designation of '*Moore*' were interchangeable for the original author of the underlying script, and it is up to the editor to choose between the designators.

In the First Folio text, set from Q3 but also drawing upon another manuscript source, there is a conspicuous regularizing effort regarding character names: as Gary Taylor notes, we see a shift 'from quarto '*Moore*' to Folio '*Aron*', from '*Queene*' to '*Tamora*', and from '*King*' and '*Emperor*' to '*Sat.*'.[33] However, even those changes were introduced inconsistently, with the speech prefix '*Moore*' still used in some scenes (e.g., dd3ʳ; and, similarly, '*King*' is still used for Saturninus on dd2ʳ). In Bate's edition the character is regularized as 'AARON' for all speech prefixes, yet, and curiously, he retains a variant designation when substantively reproducing stage directions from his copy text (Q1). The Latin cue for Aaron to remain onstage is rendered by Bate as '*Exeunt all except the Moor*' and thereafter 'AARON' speaks. For a modern reader, there is little confusion as the first referent must signal the second for the only character onstage; that is, '*the Moor*' must be 'AARON', replicating the Q1 arrangement – but the regularization of all subsequent speech prefixes to the personal name conceals the authorial activity that uses the identifiers interchangeably. A form of 'Aaron', followed by 'eds since Rowe' and therefore long established, is thus justified by Bate for the character's name. But was 'Moor', the alternative form found repeatedly in the earliest printing, closest to the papers,

Taylor and Loughnane, 'The Canon and Chronology of Shakespeare's Works' in Gary Taylor and Gabriel Egan, eds., *New Oxford Shakespeare: Authorship Companion* (Oxford: Oxford University Press, 2017), pp. 490–493.

33 Gary Taylor, 'Introduction' to *Titus Andronicus*, ed. Gary Taylor, Terri Bourus, Rory Loughnane, Anna Pruitt, and Francis X. Connor, *New Oxford Shakespeare: Critical Reference Edition*, Vol. 1 (Oxford: Oxford University Press, 2017), p. 138.

considered as an option? There are of course very significant political reasons for not identifying a character in a modern edition, and a villainous character at that, as an ethnic or racialized type rather than an individual with a proper name.[34] Yet the editorial activity here renders mostly invisible the ethno-racial politics documented by the quarto text. None of this is to say that Bate chose wrongly in introducing 'AARON' as his preferred regular form. Rather, we want to draw attention to the fact that this was an editorial *choice*, and one left unexplained, and that such choices may impact upon our reading experience and understanding of this play and others. Aaron's progress beyond a type – and he is never simply a type in the way that the Clown in the same play is – is most fully established by editorial convention.

When editing the plays of Shakespeare, we are (in almost all instances) editing a version of his dramatic writing at least one step removed from the author himself. This is because Shakespeare's plays are preserved (almost entirely) in print rather than manuscript. For the names of characters, as with all elements of the text, we are then dependent upon the accuracy of the compositor and their fidelity to an underlying manuscript. That underlying manuscript may, of course, be several further steps removed from Shakespeare's own hand. The only passage of dramatic writing in Shakespeare's own hand is the first of his three additions to the manuscript of *The Booke of Sir Thomas More* (Harley MS 7368); the other two likely Shakespearean additions to the play are preserved in transcriptions made by the so-called Hand C, an

---

[34] On Aaron and the racial politics of this early tragedy, see, for example: Ayanna Thompson, 'The Racial Body and Revenge: *Titus Andronicus*', *Textus: English Studies in Italy*, 13,2 (2000), 325–346; Ania Loomba's chapter on 'Wilderness and Civilization in *Titus Andronicus*', in *Shakespeare, Race, and Colonialism*, Oxford Shakespeare Topics (Oxford: Oxford University Press, 2002), pp. 75–90; Noémie Ndiaye, 'Aaron's Roots: Spaniards, Englishmen, and Blackamoors in *Titus* Andronicus', *Early Theatre* 19,2 (2016): 59–80; and David Sterling Brown, '"Is Black so Base a Hue?": Black Life Matters in Shakespeare's *Titus Andronicus*', in Cassander L. Smith, Nicholas R. Jones and Miles P. Grier, eds., *Early Modern Black Diaspora Studies: A Critical Anthology*, (New York: Palgrave Macmillan, 2018), pp. 137–155.

unknown scribe (Additions III and V). All of Shakespeare's other plays, or parts of plays, are only preserved in print, where the nature of alteration to the text, including with character names, is challenging if not impossible to firmly establish. Thus, Addition IIc (i.e., the third section of Addition II) in *Sir Thomas More*, in Shakespeare's autograph, represents our best documentary evidence for the author's habitual working practices in identifying characters by name in stage directions and speech prefixes.[35] The impression left behind is largely one of carelessness with respect to character names. Shakespeare's addition must be heavily annotated by Hand C to produce a workable text for performance. As John Jowett observes in his Arden 3 edition:

> [Hand C] noted both the vagueness of some of Shakespeare's [speech prefixes] and the absence of speeches assigned to particular roles. He altered eight [speech prefixes], thus securing roles for Clown Betts and Williamson, whom Shakespeare had not identified at all.[36]

These eight altered speech prefixes reward further consideration. For the first four, Shakespeare had simply written a variation of 'Other' (for non-determined speakers) in the margin, for which Hand C then distinguished specific speakers (in order, George Betts ('Geo bett'), Clown Betts ('betts clow'), Williamson ('willian'), and Clown Betts ('Clown. Betts') again). Next, Hand C altered Shakespeare's 'Sher' to 'maior'; Shakespeare's speech prefix produces an ambiguity as it could be a slip for 'Shre', indicating Shrewsbury, the mayor, or be short for 'Sheriff' which would indicate the speaker as Sir Thomas More. (More is, perhaps notably, identified as 'Moor' or 'moo' in speech prefixes.) Further contributing to these ambiguities, a speech three lines later is assigned by Shakespeare to 'Sher', where it must refer to 'Sherwin', a rebel figure. Shakespeare's inserted passage also omits

---

[35] Addition IIc is a three-page scene (ff. 8r, 8v, and 9r), which equates to the first 165 lines of Scene 6 of the play. It depicts an insurrection scene that carefully envelops humour within its threat of imminent violence.

[36] John Jowett, ed. *Sir Thomas More*, The Arden Shakespeare Third Series (London: Methuen Drama, 2011), p. 382.

an entrance direction.[37] Shakespeare's insertion thus begins with a speech
from a character identified in the left margin as 'Lincolne'; thereafter for that
character it is a game of diminishing returns for the designation of this
character: 'Linco', 'Linc', 'Lin', 'Lin', and so on. (Shakespeare's use of
'Other' follows a similar pattern: 'other', 'oth', 'o'). The apparent carelessness may then be in part explained by the fact that Shakespeare expected that
someone else would tidy up his passage to make it cohere with the rest of the
revised manuscript; that overall revision work appears to have been coor-
dinated by Hand C. (The repeated use of the non-prescriptive, and therefore unresolved, 'other' precludes any other possibility.) Shakespeare's
naming practices in *Sir Thomas More* may, therefore, be slightly unusual,
even out of character.

Recent work on playhouse manuscripts by Tiffany Stern and Paul
Werstine, the former describing the relationship between the various forms
of performance documents, including authorial drafts, the backstage-plots,
actors' parts, and other stage documents, and the latter demolishing the new
bibliographers' distinctions between authorial 'foul papers' and theatrical
'prompt books', has helped reveal the ways in which character names came
to populate and vary between different forms of documents. In plotting
a play – that is, outlining what happens in a play scene-by-scene before its
composition – dramatists would have had to identify, by name, which
characters appeared when. In selling a play to a company, based upon the
plot or draft, the dramatist would have to be able to state how many actors
were needed and the sorts of roles each named character represented. Moving
to the playhouse setting, Stern notes the importance of the list of 'persons' or
characters for casting, part creation, revision, and cutting.[38] Distinguishing
which character is speaking and when would have been of singular importance in creating the set of documents required to rehearse and perform the
play. At the very least, the characters needed to be recognizably individuated

---

[37] This is because, as Jowett notes, the entrance direction is supplied at the end of
the earlier-written Scene 5, added by Hand C at the foot of fol. 7b, and 'designed
to assist Shakespeare' as a prompt for the scene to be written (p. 379).

[38] See Tiffany Stern, *Documents of Performance in Early Modern England*
(Cambridge: Cambridge University Press, 2009).

to allow the creation of parts. Actors would have received their part, a roll containing their speech cues from other characters and their own speeches to memorize.[39] The character's name, or one version of it, must have headed the roll, allowing for identification of part and reuse. Werstine's analysis of nineteen play manuscripts and three quartos marked up for performance, demonstrates that 'All kinds of theatrical texts – MS or printed, scribal or authorial – exhibit both variation and ambiguity in naming'.[40] The sort of variation in naming we find in IIc of *Sir Thomas More*, an autograph copy marked up by a scribe, is to be expected at all stages of the transmission of the text; interestingly, the only time in which such variation is entirely unconfusing is in the actor's prepared part. As that document is for a single actor to rehearse, it is more important that the other content in the roll, the cues and dialogue, is correctly ordered. In other words, in the playhouse performance space, it does not matter whether their dialogue is preceded by a variant speech prefix; all they would be remembering are their cues to speak and the speech to follow.

With variation in character names and forms a given in playhouse manuscripts, what implications does that hold for printed playbooks? For Werstine, such variation could be introduced at any stage: authorial composition and revision, scribal, playhouse annotation, and printshop alterations. R. B. McKerrow, in an influential study, argued that variation in names in a playhouse manuscript would be *necessarily* emended by a bookkeeper to avoid ambiguity.[41] But Werstine's study rejects this thesis: 'There are ... plenty of indications in playhouse [manuscripts] of bookkeepers reaching into [stage directions] and [speech prefixes] (which do see print) to introduce multiple designations of characters of the kind McKerrow thought theatrical personnel

---

[39] See Simon Palfrey and Tiffany Stern, *Shakespeare in Parts* (Oxford: Oxford University Press, 2007), esp. pp. 15–24.

[40] Paul Werstine, *Early Modern Playhouse Manuscripts and the Editing of Shakespeare* (Oxford: Oxford University Press, 2012), p. 150.

[41] McKerrow surmises that 'a copy intended for use in the theatre would surely, of necessity, be accurate and unambiguous in the matter of character-names'. R. B. McKerrow, 'A Suggestion Regarding Shakespeare's Manuscripts', *The Review of English Studies*, 11,44 (1935): 464 (459–465).

would instead expunge'.[42] Thus, variation in naming is no longer considered a reliable guide to the provenance of the manuscript underlying a printed playbook. This is of special importance for criticism, where variation in naming for certain characters was thought to reveal Shakespeare's understanding of that character. McKerrow and Werstine observe the example of the changing designator for Lady Capulet, including, in speech prefixes alone, variations of '*Wife*', '*Capulet's Wife*', '*Lady*', '*Old Lady*', and '*Mother*'. McKerrow supposed the variation showed Shakespeare's intentions; Werstine counters that 'it becomes impossible to assume that any particular [speech prefix] must be authorial just because it is irregular'.[43] While Stern's work reveals the importance of character designation, and its practical utility for rehearsal and performance, Werstine's arguments unsettle existing ideas about how character designation and character action might intersect by highlighting the challenges involved in assigning authorial agency.

Character names thus emerge as an important locus for our understanding of the transmission of materials within the playhouse setting and from manuscript to print. There is variation in naming introduced by authors, including consistency errors (e.g., a 'Count' identified as a 'Duke', etc.), that might emerge organically in the heat of writing. There is also variation that might be introduced by authors that might be understood in a more creative way; that is, that the variation betrays how the author is thinking about or framing the character in a distinctive way during composition (e.g., the solitary use of 'Harry' in *2 Henry IV*). Here variation is not intended in the sense that the author wishes to foreground the alternative designator they are using. Rather, if inherited from autograph copy, it is a variation in practice that reflects how the author is conceiving of the character at the time of writing. But, as ever, there remains uncertainty about the source of the variation, and how heavily mediated the copy is underlying the printed text. While the author remains the most likely agent of systematic variation in character names, an attentive

---

[42] Werstine, *Early Modern Playhouse Manuscripts*, p. 150. Werstine first addressed McKerrow's assumptions in a chapter-length study, 'McKerrow's "Suggestion" and Twentieth-Century Textual Criticism' *Renaissance Drama*, New Series, 19 (1988): 149–173.

[43] Werstine, *Early Modern Playhouse Manuscripts*, pp. 154–155.

editor needs to understand that variation could be introduced by several means.

In concluding this section, we must consider also the issue of naming variation in the creative setting of the playhouse to reassess the relationship between character (the individual to be enacted), part (the speeches and cues for action assigned to the actor playing that character), and character name or names (how the character played by the actor is identified in the unspoken paratextual materials in playhouse manuscripts, character lists, stage directions, speech prefixes, and in the spoken dialogue of the play). We know character names were changed for reasons of censorship but were they ever changed in rehearsal? For characters with multiple designators, were they also designated variously in the other playhouse documents created for performance? How intertwined, in other words, were character and character names? And might the editorial impetus to regularize obscure a more flexible attitude towards names and naming within a playhouse setting?

In the fast-paced Jack Cade scenes of *2 Henry VI*, there are two characters, Lord Scales and Matthew Gough, who are identified by name in stage directions but never addressed by name in the play. At the beginning of scene 17, the stage direction reads '*Enter Lord Scales vpon the Tower walking. Then enters two or three Citizens below*'. Over the twelve lines of dialogue of the scene, Scales is never identified by name. An audience would therefore not know who he is. Scales says to the citizens that he will send them '*Matthew Goffe*', and the scene ends. Following a short scene featuring Cade and his cronies at London stone, scene 19 opens with this direction: '*Alarums. Matthew Goffe is slain, and all the rest*'. The problem is that the audience do not know who Gough is of those slain as he had never been introduced before. These problems are far from insurmountable in performance, of course, and it may be that the scenes in the Folio text have been cut in some way that accidentally introduced these uncertainties for performance. Or there may have been an abandoned intention on the dramatist's part to develop these characters more fully. For readers, and therefore editors, there is no difficulty in comprehension, while for audiences these two characters are simply anonymous. We introduce this example, therefore, not to highlight an editorial predicament but rather to demonstrate a more relaxed attitude towards naming in performance conditions. This example furthermore reminds us of the very real difference between reading and watching a play, and how what we hear and see on the stage, with its aural and visual effects (e.g., voice, costumes), may be different to that which is in the text underlying the performance. Textual problems are not always theatrical problems.

Rowe's commitment to regularizing Shakespeare's plays, one entirely in line with Tonson's house style in the early eighteenth century, has influenced editorial practice for early modern drama in the 300 years since. While his set of practices helped make the plays more readily accessible through the conventions it established, the decision-making underlying his practices of regularization remained opaque. Such opaqueness is a problem that continues to haunt editorial work today as the regularization of, say, certain character names in certain forms have been introduced but not explained. Past choices become ossified through the editorial tradition. Such a choice may remain the right choice but any editorial decision that impacts upon how a reader understands the text they are reading, analysing, teaching, performing, and so on, needs to be defended. Editorial conservatism breeds editorial malaise, a position of weakness. Editing Shakespeare is always re-editing Shakespeare, and it is not only the Shakespearean text that needs to be approached with fresh eyes but also the history of editorial decision-making.

2 Archipelagic Encounters

J. A. Froude was sure that Shakespeare drew his Celtic characters from life: 'Fluellen, Captain Jamie, and Captain Macmorris were the typical Welshman, Scot, and Irishman, as they were to be met with in Elizabeth's trainbands'.[44] This section assesses the archipelagic experience in Shakespeare's London, both within and outside the playhouse. The goal here is not to be exhaustive but rather exemplary, highlighting the sorts of hitherto underexplored connections to be found between archipelagic identities and London's commercial

---

[44] J. A. Froude, *The English in Ireland in the Eighteenth Century*, 2 Vols. (New York: Scribner, Armstrong, 1873), I, p. 7.

stage. If we are to explore the how and why of where Shakespeare borrowed his specific archipelagic names from – which would later become ossified through an editorial tradition committed to regularization – we need first to understand how the dramatist might be exposed to archipelagic matters through his daily business. Here we describe some of the Irish, Scottish, and Welsh figures connected with the early professional theatrical scene, including actors, patrons, and writers, to better understand Shakespeare's creative environment and borrowings.

Let us begin with those from Ireland. Mark Eccles notes a William Mago (1579–1632), 'also spelled Maygowe and probably stressed on the second syllable, may be a form of some Irish surname such as Magaw'.[45] Eccles mentions another actor, Emanuel Reade, moving to Ireland after 1616.[46] Elizabethan actors were active in Ireland earlier: 'In the *Ancient Treasury Book of the City of Dublin* it is noted for the year 1589 that £4 were to be paid to the "queens players for shewing their sports" and also to the "queen an Earl of Essex players"'.[47] E. K. Chambers notes that the Duke of York's Men, who became the Prince Charles's Men in 1612, were at Youghal in east Cork on 11 February 1615.[48] This raises the question as to which other players made that crossing, and vice versa.

In Thomas Brown's *Wit for money* (1691), when the poet Stutter laments how his poem was sung by a ballad-singer in the streets who 'murders it as much as a bad *Irish* Actor a good part'.[49] But were there good Irish actors? W. J. Lawrence suggested that in Shakespeare's day 'a host of adventurous Munster Gaels had made their way somehow to London to earn a precarious

---

[45] Mark Eccles, 'Elizabethan Actors III: K–R', *Notes and Queries* 39, 3 (1992): 297 (293–303). Mago played in *The Witch of Edmonton* and *Believe as You List* (297–298). Mago's 'father John built the stage and galleries of the Boar's Head in 1599'. Andrew Gurr, *The Shakespeare Company, 1594–1642* (Cambridge: Cambridge University Press, 2004), p. 235.

[46] Eccles, 'Elizabethan Actors III: K–R', 301.

[47] Peter Kavanagh, *The Irish Theatre: Being a History of the Drama in Ireland from the Earliest Period up to the Present Day* (Tralee: The Kerryman), p. 12.

[48] E. K. Chambers, *The Elizabethan Stage*, II (Oxford: Oxford University Press, 1923), p. 244.

[49] Thomas Brown, *Wit for Money, or, Poet Stutter* (London: 1691), p. 23.

living as costermongers, chimney-sweeps, and running footmen'.[50] There were
certainly real Irish characters in London as well as dramatic ones.[51] One
possibly useful category of information might be the presence of (Irish)
Gaelic in play-scripts: if we reason that there was a Welsh speaker around so
that Lady Mortimer can say actual words rather than gibberish, and further
suppose that he may have been a member of the company (playing Sir Hugh
Evans, etc.), then the incidence of Gaelic might bear the same inference. What
we have, limiting it to cases where it is specifically Irish and not Scots or
generic Gaelic, is: Heywood(?)'s *Stukeley* in 1596 (Admiral's Men); *Henry V* in
1599 (Chamberlain's Men); Dekker's *2 The Honest Whore* in 1605 (Prince's Men,
i.e., former Admiral's); Jonson, Chapman, and Marston's *Eastward Ho!* in 1605
(Children of the Queen's Revels); Beaumont and Fletcher's *The Coxcomb* in
1609 (Children of the Whitefriars, i.e., former Children of the Queen's Revels);
Middleton and Rowley's *A Fair Quarrel*, B-Text, in 1616 (Prince Charles's
Men); Dekker's *The Welsh Ambassador* in 1623 (Lady Elizabeth's Men); and
Jonson's *The New Inn* in 1629 (King's Men). The play that is probably most
significant for our purposes is *Stukeley*, where Q prints two variant versions of
scene 7, one in standard English and the other in pseudo-Irish, with some Gaelic.
How the play's author(s) (Heywood? with a collaborator?) gained some working knowledge of Gaelic is unknown, but we need not necessarily assume they
learned it from an encounter in London.[52] A later example may reveal how such
a transfer of knowledge could occur. As noted, Prince Charles' Men were in
Youghal in 1615. A year later, the company staged *A Fair Quarrel*. The author of
the B-text scene with the Gaelic was actor-playwright William Rowley who
may have picked up the language across the Irish Sea.[53]

---

[50] W. J. Lawrence, 'The Mystery of Lodowick Barry', *Studies in Philology* 14, 2
(1917): 52 (52–63).

[51] W. J. Lawrence, 'Was Shakespeare ever in Ireland? A Conjectural Study',
Shakespeare Jahrbuch 42 (1906): 69 (65–75).

[52] See Stephen O'Neill, 'Ireland onstage in *Captain Thomas Stukeley*', in *Staging
Ireland*, pp. 118–142.

[53] We are grateful to Martin Wiggins for his helpful feedback about stage Gaelic
(personal correspondence). Our study follows the chronological arrangements
proposed in these two studies: Gary Taylor and Rory Loughnane, 'The Canon

An Irish captain is a cut above the usual run of Elizabethan Irish characters: 'Save in the very early plays, the Irish characters are drawn from the lower classes of London-Irish of the time, footmen, porters, beggars or clever rogues'.[54] Exceptions include 'Gillamor, King of Ireland' in *The Misfortunes of Arthur* (1588) and 'the rich King of Hibernia' in *King Leir* (1589).[55] In 1599, Irish characters appear in Munday, Drayton, Wilson, and Hathway's *Sir John Oldcastle* and *Henry V*; and in Dekker's *Old Fortunatus* two characters pretend to be Irish costermongers. These speak dialect and appear to be comic intention, although as we shall see the use of dialect in the drama of the period suggests subversion as well as containment. There are other speaking parts in, as we have seen, *Stukeley* (1596), *2 The Honest Whore* (1608), *The Coxcomb* (1609), Jonson's *Irish Masque* (1613) and *Bartholomew Fair* (1614), Heywood's *The Four Prentices of London* (1615), *A Fair Quarrel* (1616) and *The Welsh Ambassador* (1623), *The New Inn* (1629), and Thomas Randolph's *Hey for Honesty, Down with Knavery* (*c.* 1627). Bartley describes five kinds of stage Irishmen: 'swaggering Ireland captains', tradesmen, footmen, beggars, and 'wild Irish' or kerns.[56]

and Chronology of Shakespeare's Works' in Gary Taylor and Gabriel Egan, eds., *New Oxford Shakespeare: Authorship Companion* (Oxford: Oxford University Press, 2017), pp. 417–602, for Shakespeare's works; and the multiple volumes of Martin Wiggins in association with Catherine Richardson, *British Drama, 1533–1642: A Catalogue* (Oxford: Oxford University Press, 2012), for other plays and entertainments.

54 H. Macaulay FitzGibbon, 'Ireland and the Irish in the Elizabethan Drama', *The Irish Monthly* 56, 665 (1928): 593 (589–595).

55 *The true chronicle history of King Leir* (London: 1605), A3ᵛ. FitzGibbon, 'Ireland and the Irish in the Elizabethan Drama', pp. 589–290. See Thomas Hughes, *The Misfortunes of Arthur*, in John W. Cunliffe, ed., *Early English Classical Tragedies* (Oxford: Clarendon Press, 1912), pp. 220–296.

56 J. O. Bartley, 'The Development of a Stock Character I. The Stage Irishman to 1800', *The Modern Language Review* 37, 4 (1942): 440 (438–447). Bartley lists the three Irish captains in a note: 'Respectively, Macmorris (*Henry V*), Whit (*Bart. Fair*), and Albo (*Fair Quarrel*)', 440, n.3.

There were also a few Irish fools making a living, and if we broaden the Elizabethan stage to include the Irish theatre of war, we find some fascinating figures. Essex's successor as Lord Deputy in Ireland, Sir Charles Blount, Lord Mountjoy, kept an Irish fool called Neale Moore during his campaign there.[57] Fynes Moryson's recollection of Moore suggests that Irish clowning had a sly aspect; 'wee found him to haue craft of humoring euery man to attayne his owne endes, and to haue nothing of a naturall foole'.[58] Mountjoy may of course be the 'Generall . . ./ from Ireland comming,/ Bringing Rebellion broached on his Sword' (*Henry V*, 5.30–32).[59] If so, then it is striking that this same general had a performance of *Gorboduc* staged at Dublin Castle on 7 September 1601 (Queen Elizabeth's birthday).[60] Mountjoy and Essex had together attended a performance of *Comedy of Errors* in 1594.[61] Christopher Morash imagines the succession play being performed with its audience of English viceroy and Irish fool.[62]

What of Welsh characters? Joan Rees points to the historical as well as linguistic environment Shakespeare inhabited, and detects a decline in Shakespeare's regard for the Welsh from Glendower through Fluellen to Parson Evans.[63] Gary Taylor sees Shakespeare as blazing a trail with his

[57] Alan J. Fletcher, *Drama, Performance, and Polity in Pre-Cromwellian Ireland* (Cork: Cork University Press, 2000), p. 226.

[58] Fletcher, *Drama, Performance, and Polity*, p. 226. Earlier English chief governors in Ireland kept Irish fools among their entourage, including Walter Devereux, whose fool was called 'James' (p. 222). Fletcher surmises that the fool who followed Henry Sidney in Ireland – Will (Sheyntton) – may have been an Englishman (p. 217).

[59] For Mountjoy's candidacy see Richard Dutton, '"Methinks the Truth Should Live from Age to Age": The Dating and Contexts of *Henry V*', *Huntington Library Quarterly* 68, 1–2 (2005): esp. 196–200 (173–204).

[60] Fletcher, *Drama, Performance, and Polity*, pp. 225–256.

[61] Fletcher, *Drama, Performance, and Polity*, p. 226.

[62] Christopher Morash, *A History of Irish Theatre, 1601–2000* (Cambridge: Cambridge University Press, 2002), p. 3.

[63] Joans Rees, 'Shakespeare's Welshmen', *Literature and Nationalism*, eds. Vincent Newey and Ann Thompson (Liverpool: Liverpool University Press, 1991), p. 38 (pp. 22–40).

Welsh characters as 'the first Elizabethan dramatist to attempt a Welsh accent'.[64] For F. J. Harries the Welsh captain slotted into a tradition of sympathetic figures from that country, noting that 'Shakespeare's Welshmen are all good men and true' (listing Henry V, Henry VII, Glendower, Sir Hugh Evans, the Welsh Captain, and Belarius) and that among them, 'Fluellen is loyal and chivalrous'.[65] This view asks us to overlook the subversive quality of Fluellen. For Harries, Fluellen stood out as another Welsh figure to be regarded favourably, not as an object of ridicule: 'Indeed, we may claim Shakespeare as a champion of Welsh nationality, for in *King Henry V*, the fiery Fluellen makes an English braggart eat the leek, while Gower severely admonishes Pistol for ridiculing the Welsh'.[66] Others have not been so certain about this, and, as we shall see in a later section on how Fluellen's name and nature may conceal historical and political ballast. More certainly, the transmission of Shakespeare's most famous Welsh character owes in part to Welsh support: two Welsh brothers, the Herberts, are celebrated dedicatees of the First Folio.

Turning to Scottish influences, it is worth revisiting the years leading up to *Henry V*'s first performance to finesse our understanding of the Scottish reaction to English drama. Scottish anti-theatricality has been exaggerated.[67]

---

[64] Gary Taylor, ed., *Henry V* (Oxford: Clarendon Press, 1982), p. 161, note to 3.2.19. Taylor observes that 'stage Welshmen also appear in *Patient Grissel* (1600), *Satiromastix* (1601), *Northward Ho* (1605), and *The Welsh Ambassador* (c.1623), all by Dekker, and in *Sir John Oldcastle* (1599), which seems indebted in several respects to *Henry V*. None of these consistently reproduces the accent, and all of Dekker's display the same characteristics (so parallels have usually been cited in only one or two)'.

[65] Frederick J. Harries, *Shakespeare and the Welsh* (London: T. Fisher Unwin, 1919), p. 68.

[66] Harries, *Shakespeare and the Welsh*, pp. 65–66.

[67] See Andrew Murphy, who notes that 'regular performances of Shakespeare were uncommon [in Scotland] before the end of the 18th century', in Dobson and Wells, eds., *The Oxford Companion to Shakespeare*, p. 484 (pp. 483–484). For its lively theatrical culture, see Michael Bath, '"Rare Shewes and Singular Inventions": The Stirling Baptism of Prince Henry', *Journal of the Northern Renaissance* 4 (2012): 1 (1–16) and Bill Findlay, 'Performances and Plays', in

Popular drama in sixteenth-century Scotland was a lively affair: 'Robin Hood plays were ... extremely popular with children and adults alike, and to judge by the number of times they had to be banned, they constituted a threat to civil and church authority'.[68] The Scottish reputation for stage censorship has also been exaggerated.[69] On a visit to Aberdeen in 1562 Mary Queen of Scots was greeted with 'spectacles, plays, and interludes'.[70] Indeed, the national stereotype of dour anti-theatricality has obscured the performance politics of the time. When Mary's grandson, Henry, appeared on the scene his birth was marked by 'generously rewarded' English actors.[71] According to William Fowler, who oversaw the dramatic celebrations at Stirling for Prince Henry's baptism alongside Patrick Leslie (Lord Lindores), 'those exercises, that wer to

Ian Brown, Thomas Clancy, Susan Manning and Murray Pittock, eds., *The Edinburgh History of Scottish Literature: From Columba to the Union (until 1707)* (Edinburgh: Edinburgh University Press, 2007), p. 253 (pp. 253–262).

[68] Meradith T. McMunn, 'Children as Actors and Audience for Early Scottish Drama and Ceremony', *Children's Literature Association Quarterly* 10, 1 (1985): 22 (22–24).

[69] Keith Brown, 'Historical Context and *Henry V*', *Cahiers Élisabéthains* 29, 1 (1986): 79–80. Brown describes 'the interesting fact of the Scottish royal family's friendliness and relative generosity to English players. (Predictably, every reference to an *Ur*-Hamlet is in a year of major public importance in Anne of Denmark's married life.) And the visits of English actors – in Scotland again in both 1598 and 1599 – afforded a natural channel for gossip about the Scottish court: Gossip to which Shakespeare demonstrably listened at times'.

[70] J. Keith Angus, *A Scotch Playhouse; Being the Historical Records of the Old Theatre Royal, Marischal Street, Aberdeen* (Aberdeen: D. Wyllie & Son, 1878), p. 13. See also Sarah Carpenter, 'Performing Diplomacies: The 1560s Court Entertainments of Mary Queen of Scots', *Scottish Historical Review* 82, 2 (2003): 218 (194–225). Like Shakespeare's Henry V, Mary wondered what it would be like to pass for a mere man: 'The queen was also recorded as alert to cross-gender experience, reportedly wishing she were a man "to know what life it was to lie all night in fields, or to walk upon the causeway with a jack and knapscall"' A 'knapscall' was a defensive headpiece or metal skullcap.

[71] Peter R. Roberts, 'The Business of Playing and the Patronage of Players at the Jacobean Courts', in Ralph Houlbrooke, ed., *James VI and I: Ideas, Authority, and Government* (Aldershot: Ashgate, 2006), p. 85 (pp. 81–105).

be vsed for decoration of that solemnitie, were to be deuided both in Feeld pastimes, with Martiall and heroicall exploites, and in houshold, with rare shewes and singular inventions'.[72]

Who were the English actors at the Stirling baptism of Prince Henry? According to Peter Roberts:

> That this troupe was led by Lawrence Fletcher is suggested
> by James's badinage with George Nicholson, secretary to
> the English ambassador in Edinburgh, as reported by him
> a year later, on 22 March 1595, to Robert Bowes at the
> garrison at Berwick: the king heard that Fletcher, the player,
> was hanged, and told me and [the Scottish courtier] Roger
> Ashton so, in merry words, not believing it, saying very
> pleasantly that if it were true he would hang them also.[73]

This merriment was short-lived if we take at face value the report that James was dismayed by the conduct of English players three years later. In the spring of 1598 'the Comediens of London' had apparently caused a stir north of the Border with some perceived anti-Scottish material. Roberts established that the complaint, such as it was, centred on a performance in Edinburgh, and not, as Chambers had assumed, one staged in London.[74] Roberts goes on to point out that when the Scottish clergy objected to a subsequent visit by an English troupe James overturned their opinion.[75] Roberts notes that Robert Bruce, the

---

[72] William Fowler, *A True Reportarie of [. . .] the Baptisme of the Most Excellent, Right High, and Mightie Prince, Frederik Henry* (Edinburgh: 1594), A4ʳ.

[73] Roberts, 'The Business of Playing and the Patronage of Players at the Jacobean Courts', 85. The entry in the *Calendar of the State Papers Relating to Scotland* gives Aston's name correctly: 'The King heard that Fletcher, the player, was hanged, and told him and Roger Aston so, in merry words, not believing it, saying very pleasantly that if it were true he would hang them also' (London: Longman, 1858), II, p. 676.

[74] Roberts, 'The Business of Playing and the Patronage of Players at the Jacobean Courts', pp. 85–86.

[75] Roberts, 'The Business of Playing and the Patronage of Players at the Jacobean Courts', p. 86. Earlier critics pondered whether Shakespeare accompanied

Kirk's 'most outspoken minister', insisted upon the right to warn the godly against the English players: 'we have good reasoun to stay them from their playes, even by your owne acts of parliament'. James asserted his authority – comedians were to be allowed freely to enjoy the benefit of their royal warrant – and the incident reflected his growing confidence in dealing with the Kirk as well as his resolve to be seen to be on good terms with England at this time.

Carpenter notes the extent to which theatre flourished even in post-Reformation Scotland with royal support:

> James VI showed interest in this new English drama and in 1599 was instrumental in enabling a company of English players to set up a playhouse and perform publicly in Edinburgh. ... James' departure for London two years later left commercial players without a patron powerful enough to promote their cause.[76]

In October 1599, there is a note of '£43, 6s. and 8d. to be given by the King to the English comedians'.[77] Fletcher was still acting for James in 1607 when he appears in a list of 'Players of Enterludes'. Royal resistance to clerical censoriousness makes of James VI a fitting match for the player king. For Bill Findlay, 'such royal protection and patronage of theatre was lost with the removal of James to London in 1603 on his accession to the English throne', and James's departure for London marks the end of a fruitful theatrical tradition, but the Stuarts played a key role in court culture in London.[78]

Fletcher. See Charles Knight, 'Did Shakespere Visit Scotland?', in *William Shakespeare: A Biography*, 3rd ed. (London: George Routledge and Sons, 1867), pp. 419–464.

[76] Sarah Carpenter, 'Scottish Drama until 1650', in Ian Brown, ed., *The Edinburgh Companion to Scottish Drama* (Edinburgh: Edinburgh University Press, 2011), pp. 20–21 (pp. 6–21). See also Anna Jean Mill, *Mediaeval Plays in Scotland* (Edinburgh: Blackwood, 1927), p. 110. On James's subsequent patronage of the theatre, see E. K. Chambers, 'Court Performances under James the First', *The Modern Language Review* 4,2 (1909): 153–166.

[77] Mill, *Mediaeval Plays in Scotland*, p. 300.

[78] Findlay, 'Performances and Plays', p. 257.

Indeed, two relatively obscure Stuart brothers, Ludovic, Duke of Lennox, and Esmé, Lord Aubigny, were promoters of Jacobean drama.[79]

Any of these archipelagic leads – from actors and characters to officers and patrons – might be pursued to tag further links between the experience of living in a multi-nation archipelago and the ways in which that experience manifests in stage representations. Our goal here is to highlight the fluidity and instability of these Anglo-Celtic connections and corrections in terms of the contested nature of naming as an interplay between colonial appropriation and native resistance. Names are never neutral and editorial practice should be alert to this fact. This is starkly at odds with the editorial mission to fix such archipelagic identities in terms of its regularizing naming practices.

3 Four Names

In this section, we map out the whereabouts and trace the origins and afterlives of Shakespeare's four captains, moving back and forward in time from the fifteenth through to the eighteenth centuries to determine what factors and forces brought these officers of Wales, England, Scotland, and Ireland together on a field in France in 1415 as seen in a play staged in 1599. This scene, ripe for a discussion of naming and nationhood, is often omitted in performance, or, just as bad, quartered by critics so that the singular focus is on the Irish captain, with the others mere supporting actors. Here we home in on four figures who can be read as representatives of a nascent archipelagic state, but also, and more complexly, as characters whose names and nations, far from defining them, raise crucial questions around theatres of war and empire in the period, and highlight the ways in which drama and history interact.

The Welsh Captain

Fluellen, for let us identify him by his traditional name for now, is not Shakespeare's first Welsh captain. A precursor appears briefly in *Richard II* 2.4 at a camp in Wales where he delivers a speech as princely and prophetic

---

[79] David M. Bergeron, 'The Stuart Brothers and English Theater', in Jim Pearce and Ward J. Riswold, eds., *Renaissance Papers 2015* (2016): 1–12.

as Glendower's (Glyndŵr's or Glyn Dŵr's?) and quite unlike Fluellen's.[80]
This unnamed captain's countryman in *Henry V* has a name to conjure with:

> Fluellen ... is no neutral name – not in history, and not on the
> stage: it is a crude phonetic rendering of the Welsh 'Llewelyn,'
> the name of the last native prince of Wales ... The imagined
> community to which Fluellen belongs bears memories not only
> of its own victorious stock and native mightiness, but also of
> a specific historical moment in which those Welsh inheritances
> became a part of *English*, and not Welsh, tradition: the moment
> when the last native prince of Wales was defeated.[81]

Indeed, as Terence Hawkes outlines, it is a name, or form of name, with
complex political implications:

> Llewellyn ... can claim archetypal status. Llewellyn is the
> name of the last native Prince of Wales (Llewellyn the last).
> Moreover, fittingly, and notoriously for English ears, it deploys
> in full fig that distinctive phoneme /ll/ ... whose accurate
> pronunciation is a major Welsh shibboleth. Here, immediately
> recognisable to both Welsh and English ears, is a distinctive
> sign of Welshness. However, the initial, side-stepping and
> entirely anglicised phoneme embodied in 'Fluellen' signifies
> a language, and a highly significant name, crudely enlisted and
> in the process brutally reduced. Even more clearly than in the
> case of 'Owen Glendower', in Fluellen's name, a maimed
> linguistic ghost stirs, rattles its English cage, hints darkly at
> things that are now literally unspeakable.[82]

---

[80] This scene is discussed briefly in Arthur E. Hughes, 'Shakespeare and His Welsh
Characters', *Transactions of the Honourable Society of Cymmrodorion* (1917–1918), pp.
159–189.

[81] Marisa R. Cull, *Shakespeare's Princes of Wales: English Identity and the Welsh
Connection* (Oxford: Oxford University Press, 2014), pp. 86–87; emphasis in original.

[82] Terence Hawkes, 'Bryn Glas', *European Journal of English Studies* 1,3 (1997): 286
(269–290).

Fluellen's pronunciation has a critical edge. Hawkes notes the way in which Shakespeare editors have struggled with Fluellen's Welsh English: 'T. W. Craik offers the strange comment that "Fluellen" is "an anglicized spelling of Llewelyn (sic) that prevents incorrect pronunciation"'.[83]

Of *Henry V*'s four captains, Fluellen has the lion's share of lines: the second largest role in the entire play, speaking almost 10 per cent of the dialogue.[84] (Harry dominates, speaking nearly a third of the play's lines.) He belongs to a long tradition of Welsh performers and entertainers, and a strong tradition of Welsh themes in the drama. He also brings a double Welsh context, in terms of the origins of the Tudor dynasty and with regard to the contemporary politics of succession.[85] Joan Rees sees in Fluellen's character an expression of 'this new unity of the kingdom': 'English and Welsh hostility is now resolved and a joint nationalism claims allegiance in the person of a king who was born in Wales and professes that he too is Welsh'.[86] The Nine Years War in Ireland and the Scottish succession did not dent interest in Wales. Andrew Hiscock notes the displacement that critics engage in when trying to fit Wales into Anglo-Celtic frameworks dominated by Ireland and Scotland:

> the world of discord is that of Wales and, given this fact, some critical studies have been more than willing to impose normative schemas of cultural hierarchy. Jonson's Oxford editors, for example, note that 'like *The Irish Masque*, this Welsh Antimasque is full of lively touches of national

---

[83] Hawkes, 'Bryn Glas', p. 286, n.23. Citing T. W. Craik, ed., *Henry V*, The Arden Shakespeare (London: Routledge, 1995), p. 205.

[84] It has been suggested that casting played a part in reducing the Irish Captain's lines and inflating the Welsh Captain's. See Thomas L. Berger, 'The Disappearance of Macmorris in Shakespeare's *Henry V*', *Renaissance Papers* (1986): 13–26.

[85] See the essays by A. H. Dodd, 'Wales and the Scottish Succession', *Transactions of the Honourable Society of Cymmrodorion* Session 1937 (1938): 201–225, and A. H. Dodd, 'North Wales in the Essex Revolt of 1601', *The English Historical Review* 59, 235 (1944): 348–370.

[86] Rees, 'Shakespeare's Welshmen', p. 29.

character and speech; the flavour of the humour is not very
rich or subtle, but it is unmistakably Welsh'.[87]

Hiscock provides a useful antidote to the idea that Irish–Scottish interests
overshadowed Welsh ones, especially after the end of the Tudor dynasty
and the partial resolution of the matter of Britain: 'Throughout the Early
Modern period, Wales became frequently associated with threatening dis-
order in terms of crime, violent harassment of the English Marcher farmers,
recusancy and divided loyalties (it was viewed by contemporaries as
a possible site for invasion)'.[88]

Welsh soldiers did, however, play a major role in pacifying Ireland in
the 1590s, with Bristol, Chester, and Milford serving as departure points
and, as Robert Babcock observes, 'some 2.9 percent of the population of
Wales was called for service in Ireland' between 1594 and 1602.[89] And
Welsh soldiers had played a prominent part in earlier English military
ventures, including distinguishing themselves at Agincourt.[90] One historical Welshman who fought and died under Henry in France is Dafydd Gam,
depicted as 'a great Captaine in that Warre' in Michael Drayton's verse
account of Agincourt.[91] The comparison has a long history: 'In the valiant

---

[87] Andrew Hiscock, 'To the Honour of That Nation: Ben Jonson and the Masquing
of Wales', in Katie Gramich and Andrew Hiscock, eds., *Dangerous Diversity: The
Changing Faces of Wales* (Cardiff: University of Wales Press, 1998), p. 44
(pp. 37–63): Jonson, Shakespeare, and the Atlantic Archipelago, *Shakespeare*
12, 4 (2016): 364–374.

[88] Hiscock, 'To the Honour of That Nation', p. 50.

[89] Robert S. Babcock, '"For I Am Welsh, You Know": Henry V, Fluellen, and the
Place of Wales in the Sixteenth-Century English Nation', in James V. Mehl, ed.,
In Laudem Caroli: Renaissance and Reformation Studies for Charles G. Nauert
(Kirksville: Thomas Jefferson University Press, 1998), pp. 191–192 (pp.
189–199).

[90] Babcock, 'For I Am Welsh', p. 192. On Welsh soldiers at Agincourt see
Adam Chapman, 'The King's Welshmen: Welsh Involvement in the
Expeditionary Army of 1415', *Journal of Medieval Military History* 9 (2011): 41–64.

[91] Michael Drayton, *The Battail of Agincourt* (London: 1631), p. 41. For a sceptical
view of Gam's role see Adam Chapman, 'The Posthumous Knighting of Dafydd

and choleric Welshman, some commentators see a caricature of Davy *Gam*, which means "squint-eyed", whose real name was Llewellyn'.[92]

The view that the Scottish succession and the war in Ireland kept those countries in the news is complicated by the prominence of Wales in *Henry V*, as well as the presence of Welsh captains in Elizabeth's army in Ireland. At the Battle of the Yellow Ford in Armagh on 14 August 1598 English and Welsh forces failed to lift the siege of Blackwater Fort, where Welsh Captain Thomas Williams and a garrison of 300 men were holding out.[93] After listing Scottish allusions in Shakespeare's works, Alan Powers comments: 'Surprisingly, Welsh references are slightly higher'.[94] This only comes as a surprise because of the misconception that Wales mattered less in Shakespeare's day than Ireland or Scotland. Powers goes on to note that 'Shakespeare's works include thirty-four instances of "Wales", and twenty uses of "Welsh", all confined to the second tetralogy histories, *Henry IV, Part One, Part Two*, and *Henry V*, and a play of the same period, *The Merry Wives of Windsor*. Additionally, there are six instances of "Welshman" and five more in the plural, "Welshmen", plus the one famous use of "Welshwomen" as perpetrators of war atrocities in *Henry IV, Part One*, Act One'.[95] Welshness carried with it some peculiar connotations: 'Although an Elizabethan could not sue for being called "Welsh", it was a common modifier in defamation'.[96]

Gam', *Journal of Medieval History* 43, 1 (2017): 89–105. See also T. F. Tout, revised by R. R. Davies, 'Dafydd [David] Gam (*d*. 1415)', *ODNB*. Retrieved 19 October 2023.

[92] George Russell French, *Shakespeareana Genealogica: Identification of the Dramatis Personae in the Historic Plays, from* King John *to* Henry VIII (London and Cambridge: Macmillan, 1869), p. 105.

[93] William T. Latimer, 'The Battle of the Yellow Ford', *The Journal of the Royal Society of Antiquaries of Ireland* 10, 1 (1900): 34–39.

[94] Alan W. Powers, '"Gallia and Gaul, French and Welsh": Comic Ethnic Slander in the Gallia Wars', in Frances Teague, ed., *Acting Funny: Comic Theory and Practice in Shakespeare's Plays* (London and Toronto: Associated University Presses, 1994), p. 110 (pp. 109–122).

[95] Powers, 'Gallia and Gaul', pp. 110–111. [96] Powers, 'Gallia and Gaul', p. 111.

The Welsh Captain is much-loved; a comic, leek-carrying, larger-than-life creation, bestriding the French wars like a colossus, forcing his will, courage, and knowledge of military history upon others. But how intentional is the comedy and how far is this figure of fun bound up with the captain's reception as a Cambrian cliché? Babcock notes how the Welsh captain flits from loyal officer to buffoon: 'By butchering spoken English through the use of Welsh mutations, Fluellen, noble as his character may be, thus becomes an object of derision not dissimilar to Evans in *Merry Wives of Windsor*'.[97] Powers has an interesting take on the humorous aspect of the Welsh Captain: 'Fluellen is not the only comic Welsh character' as 'King Henry himself claims kin'.[98] Powers has in mind Henry's self-identification, 'I am Welsh' (4.7.96). The Welshness of English monarchs was a double-edged sword, of course. In John Ford's *Perkin Warbeck* (1633), James IV, backing the eponymous pretender, 'Kingly *Yorke*', pointedly calls Henry VII 'the *Welch Harrie*'.[99] For Powers, Fluellen and Henry's shared Welshness is more than a mutual capacity for wit, but a sign that Welshness itself is a source of comedy and that 'Shakespeare relies upon ethnic humour, namely dialect jokes', including making fun of French and Welsh accents.[100] Powers sees this as a paradox that is part of the play's humour: namely, the king's nationality, and suggests that laughter directed at the Welsh Captain is redeemed by Harry and the English Captain. Allison Outland views the connections between captain and king differently, as parody and bathos, arguing that from his first appearance, 'Captain Fluellen [functions] as

---

[97] Babcock, 'For I Am Welsh', p. 196.   [98] Powers, 'Gallia and Gaul', p. 117.

[99] John Ford, *The Chronicle Historie of Perkin Warbeck* (London: 1634), E1ʳ.

[100] Powers, 'Gallia and Gaul', p. 120. Fluellen's plosive play on 'big' is rehearsed in *Love's Labour's Lost* (1594):

> *Clow.* I Pompey *am*, Pompey *surnamde the bigge.*
>
> *Duma.* The great.
>
> *Clowe.* It is great sir, Pompey *surnamde the great.*
>
> *That oft in fielde with Targ and Shield did make my foe to sweat* (5.2.543–545).

Costard's quip has been used to argue that Will Kemp played both parts. See Michael D. Friedman, '"I Am but a Fool, Look You": Will Kemp and the Performance of Welshness', *Early Theatre* 25, 1(2022): 68 (57–77).

a mock or imitation of Hal as commander'.[101] Terence Hawkes has a similar take, seeing the Welsh Captain undermining the proto-British king, and unveiling in the 'Alexander the Pig' episode 'a glimpse of a potential "beastly transformation" dormant yet potent at the heart of the new Britain as corrosively as it was at the old?'[102]

Richard Levin coined the term 'Fluellenism' to cover the way certain critics push connections to the limit. This 'literary Fluellenism' leads critics up garden paths and down primrose ones:

> It is thus in the nature of things that the Fluellenist will never lack for material . . . in order to prove whatever he wants. That is the great strength of his method and also its greatest weakness.[103]

Fluellenists, for Levin, are prone to finding one-to-one correspondences between characters and historical personages.[104] Levin suggests that topical readings are influenced by the Welsh Captain's allegorical approach of 'figures and comparisons' (4.7.37), or 'the attempt to find a "historical dimension" in that drama by equating some of its characters to important contemporary personalities and particularly to King James'.[105] Levin insists 'such correspondences (or "astonishing congruences") are to be explained not by coincidence but by the industry of the Fluellenist and the special secrets of his trade . . . for this very reason, they have the same significance as the correspondence of salmon in the Wye and that river of Macedonia whose name was out of the Welshman's brains'.[106]

---

[101] Allison M. Outland, '"Eat a Leek": Welsh Corrections, English Conditions, and British Cultural Commodities', in Willy Maley and Margaret Tudeau-Clayton, eds., *This England, That Shakespeare: New Angles on Englishness and the Bard* (Farnham and Burlington: Ashgate, 2010), p. 95 (pp. 87–103).

[102] Hawkes, 'Bryn Glas', p. 287.

[103] Richard Levin, 'On Fluellen's Figures, Christ Figures, and James Figures', *PMLA* 89, 2 (1974): 303 (302–311).

[104] Levin, 'On Fluellen's Figures', p. 305.

[105] Levin, 'On Fluellen's Figures', p. 310.

[106] Levin, 'On Fluellen's Figures', p. 311.

Fluellenism is approached differently by Margaret Tudeau-Clayton, who sees in Fluellen's associationism and apparent amnesia a freighted use of historical memory, as when he remembers Falstaff's wit before his name:

> [Fluellen] remembers by reproducing one of Falstaff's habitual linguistic practices. Called 'Sinonimia or the Figure of store' by George Puttenham ... the practice is self consciously evoked by the Welsh captain ... earlier in the scene which ... significantly, introduces his overt critique of Henry's rejection of Falstaff: 'Why I pray you, is not "pig" great? The pig or the great or the mighty or the huge or the magnanimous are all one reckonings, save the phrase is a little variations' (... A practice cultivated by Renaissance humanist education 'sinonimia' ... translates diachronic change as synchronic range – the 'copia', or 'gallymafrey', of 'Englishes' that the Welshman *Flu*ellen evidently loves as much as the nomadic English courtier Falstaff and that is a function of ... the *flu*idity, we might say, of historically contingent linguistic as well as territorial boundaries.[107]

Because of Shakespeare's invention of this character, the ostensibly Welsh name of 'Fluellen' is known worldwide. Where might Shakespeare have borrowed this name from? What Welsh man or woman of the period (or the period of Henry's reign) would or could have gone by that name?[108] Most

---

[107] Margaret Tudeau-Clayton, 'Shakespeare's "welsch men" and the "King's English"', in Willy Maley and Philip Schwyzer, eds., *Shakespeare and Wales: From the Marches to the Assembly* (Farnham and Burlington: Ashgate, 2010), p. 99 (pp. 91–110); emphases in original.

[108] There's a reference, intriguing given the Welsh Captain's eye for waters, to the 'Water of Fluellen', in Konrad Gesner, *The newe iewell of health* (London: 1576), 'The Table', A7^r. See Fluellen: 'All the water in Wye, cannot wash your Maiesties Welsh plood out of your pody' (4.7.90–1). Perhaps a pun too in Gower asking: 'How now Captaine *Fluellen*, come you from the Bridge?' (3.6.1).

obviously, 'Fluellen' is Shakespeare's weak English transliteration of a Welsh family name found in a standard form as 'Llewel(l)yn' or 'Llewel(l)in'.[109] English references to 'Llewellyn' occur in Holinshed and, most notably, in Humphrey Lloyd and David Powel's *The Historie of Cambria*, and are scattered through printed works from Richard Grafton (1569) to Francis Godwin (1601).[110] The name of William Fluellen we know from the recusancy report of 1592, where he is bracketed with John Shakespeare as a church-avoider for fear of process. The burial register tells that he was buried on 9 July 1595.[111] Intriguingly, Camille Adkins notes that 'George Bardolphe' appears along with this William Fluellen on that Stratford recusancy list.[112] One untapped source in discussions of the Welsh Captain's name is Sir John Salusbury of Lleweni (1566/7–1612), one of a group of influential Elizabethan Welshmen.[113] Around the time of the printing of the early alternative version of *Henry V* (1600), John Speed prepared a map of England with a 'key' in the form of a text in four sheets pasted in the margins, including this annotation: '*At* Montgomery *Llewellin Prince of Wales through the practise of a traiterous Monke, ouercame and slew many*

---

[109] See Lisa Hopkins, 'Fluellen's Name', *Shakespeare Studies* 24 (1996): 148–155.

[110] Humphrey Lloyd and David Powel, *The Historie of Cambria, now called Wales* (London: 1584).

[111] This is earlier observed in E. K. Chambers, *William Shakespeare: A Study of Facts and Problems* (Oxford: Clarendon Press, 1930), p. 25. Gwyn Williams, 'Welshmen in Shakespeare's Stratford', *Transactions of the Honourable Society of Cymmrodorion*, Session 1954 (1955), p. 58 (pp. 31–59).

[112] Camille Adkins, 'Glendower and Fluellen; Or, Where Are the Leeks of Yesterday?', *CCTE Studies* 48 (1983): 106 (101–108).

[113] A. H. Dodd, 'North Wales in the Essex Revolt of 1601', 353 (348–370). See A. D. Carr, 'Salusbury [Salesbury] family *(per.* c. 1454–c. 1684)', *ODNB*. Retrieved 28 August 2019: 'The Lleweni estate was by [1612] one of the largest in north Wales'. As head of Lleweni Hall from 1586 Salusbury presided over a rich cultural archive. See Sally Harper, 'An Elizabethan Tune List from Lleweni Hall, North Wales', *Royal Musical Association Research Chronicle* 38, 1 (2005): 45–98.

of the Kings power. An. 1231. *reg.* H. 3.15'.[114] There was no standard form for how the name should be spelled in Welsh, or for how it should be transliterated into English. As has been observed:

> When English scribes registered the names of Welshmen,
> they had difficulty with the initial sound of *Llewellyn*, as did
> Shakespeare and others. Some of the writings employed are
> *Thelewlin, Swellin, Flewellin, Fluellen, Flawelling, Thellyn,*
> and even *Fllewelin* and *Yleulin*.[115]

How Shakespeare himself registered the name is significant. Although Floyd is found as an English form of Lloyd in the period, Shakespeare's transliteration remains unusual.[116] That Shakespeare should never have encountered this spelling in print is possible, though the name appears in sources he consulted.[117] Quite why Shakespeare adopted this unusual spelling for 'Fluellen' cannot be known. Perhaps Shakespeare remembered the name spoken aloud rather than read? Or perhaps he opted to write the name in (what he perceived to be) a phonetic version of an unfamiliar Welsh name, hoping to aid the actors in their pronunciation? (Especially given the difficulty in pronouncing the double 'll' sound – a voiceless alveolar lateral fricative.) Shakespeare, a man of the theatre writing for primarily English actors and audiences, might either hazard a guess, simplify, or do both.[118]

---

[114] John Speed, *A Description of the Ciuill Warres of England* ([S.l.: 1601?]). The Welsh and English captains appear in *Henry the fift*, predominantly identified as Flewellen and Gower; the Irish and Scottish captains do not feature.

[115] Robert A. Fowkes, 'Features of Welsh and British Celtic Onomastics', *Names: A Journal of Onomastics* 36, 3–4 (1988): 145 (143–150).

[116] Michael Drayton addressed 'Humfrey Floyd' in the preface to *Poly-olbion* entitled 'To My Friends, the Cambro-Britans'. Michael Drayton, *Poly-Olbion* (London: 1612), A1[v].

[117] 'Llewelin' is a prominent figure in the narrative of Edward I (Longshanks) in the 1577 edition of Holinshed's *Chronicles* (London: 1577).

[118] We might compare here the parallel case of Petruccio/Petruchio in *The Taming of the Shrew*. A servant in a source play of *Shrew* is called 'Petruccio' so Shakespeare had clearly encountered the name in its Italian form. He may have written Petruchio to aid English actors – that is, to signal that the 'ch' is

What is certain, is that with the name 'Fluellen', Shakespeare produces a distinctively anglicized version of a Welsh name.

But is there subterfuge at work? Shakespeare's choice of spelling may have been influenced by the popular English name for an herb, Veronica or Speedwell, that 'groweth in many places of England, and it is called in englishe Fluellyng'.[119] This herb, rendered variously as 'fluelin', 'fluellin', 'fluelling', and 'fluellyng', is commonly used as a cure for the plague (taken intravenously during blood-letting), to heal wounds (soaked in linen clothes), and diverse cures for the expurgation of 'corrupt humors'.[120] 'Fluelin' is found in a book about curing gunshot wounds received in battle.[121] Writing a history of plants, John Gerard observes of this herb, 'in Welch it is called Fluellen, and the Welch people do attribute great vertues to the same'.[122] Any connection between the herb and the character name is necessarily speculative, of course, yet we would be loath not to note 'Fluellyng/in's' conspicuously Anglophone co-option of a Welsh property and its perceived utility in scenes of combat. Not

---

to be pronounced as in English 'church'. Barbara Hodgdon identifies 'one prominent Petruccio in London, Petrucchio Ubaldini, two of whose works are plausibly associated with *Edward III*'. (See Barbara Hodgdon, ed. *The Taming of the Shrew*, Arden Third Series (London: The Arden Shakespeare, 2010), p. 136). Petruccio Ubaldini (*fl.* 1545–1599), an Italian protestant refugee who claimed Florentine citizenship, served in Ireland (he was at the Smerwick Massacre with Edmund Spenser in 1580), and assisted John Wolfe with the printing of Machiavelli's works. Ubaldini's account of the Spanish Armada, *Discourse Concerning the Spanish Fleet Invading England, in the Year 1588* (London: 1590), has been cited as a source for Act 3 of *Edward III*. (See Giorgio Melchiori, ed. *Edward III*, The New Cambridge Shakespeare (Cambridge: Cambridge University Press, 1998), p. 28.

[119] William Turner, The names of herbes in Greke, Latin, Englishe, *Duche [and] Frenche* (London: 1548), H5^r.

[120] Konrad Gesner, *The newe iewell of health* (London: 1576), p. 72^v.

[121] Joseph Du Chesne, *The Sclopotarie of Iosephus Quercetanus, phisition* (London: 1590), C2v.

[122] John Gerard, *The herball or Generall historie of plantes* (London: 1633), Bk II, p. 629. See also 'Herbe Fluelline' in Thomas Hill, *The gardeners labyrinth* (London: 1577), E2^v.

insignificantly, the *OED* notes that the English named for the herb is itself a corruption of the Welsh name for it 'Llewellyn's herb'.

The use of the spelling 'Fluellen' for a personal name, though so far unidentified in print records before Shakespeare's writing of *Henry V* in 1599, does appear in print within a generation of his death. *The History of the life, reign, and death of Edward II*, previously attributed to Henry Cary, Viscount Falkland, to Edward Fannant (on gendered assumptions), but more recently to Elizabeth Tanfield Cary (1585–1639), Viscountess Falkland, opens with an intriguing allusion to the peaceful commencement of Edward's reign: 'The principal Leaders of the Rebellious Welshmen, *Fluellen* and *Meredith*, being taken and executed, the Combustions of the *Cambro-Britains* were quieted and settled in an uniform Obedience'.[123] A Welsh soldier taken prisoner fifty years after Shakespeare's play bore the name of his dramatic countryman. An account of a parliamentary engagement in Wales included among a 'A List of the Names of the Officers taken by Col: *Horton*, May 8. 1648' an ensign named 'William Fluellen Griffeth'.[124] It is possible, even plausible, that other English writers transliterated the Welsh name as 'Fluellen', but Shakespeare's play still provides the most conspicuous example and may even have influenced the mainstream adoption of this spelling.

The English Captain

At the close of *King John*, a history play out of joint between two tetralogies, the Bastard depicts England coming out fighting from its position as the fourth corner of the world in a victory for self-determination and self-definition:

> Come the three corners of the world in arms
> And we shall shock them. Naught shall make us rue,
> If England to itself do rest but true! (5.7.116–18)

---

[123] *The History of the Life, Reign, and Death of Edward II* (London: 1680), p. 1. See Virginia Brackett, 'Elizabeth Cary, Drayton, and Edward II', *Notes and Queries* 41, 4 (1994): 517–520.

[124] Thomas Horton, *A True Confirmation of the Great Victory in Wales* (London: 1648), p. 8.

Yet England's true self was inextricably linked to its Celtic neighbours, and the untimely death of Arthur in this most English of plays did little to dampen its author's enthusiasm for the matter of Britain. Though far less prominent than his counterpart from Wales, the English Captain appears in six scenes in *Henry V*, speaking roughly 2 per cent of the dialogue. He is invariably identified as some form of '*Gower*' ('*Gow.*' or '*Gour.*' in speech prefixes). It is certainly a name with a history, and one with strong military associations. There was in fact a military figure – Sir Thomas Gower – engaged in defending the Anglo-Scottish frontier in the 1540s, and by report as argumentative as Shakespeare's Irish Captain.[125] There was also a Captain Gower serving in Ireland at the time of the early performances of Shakespeare's play. Fynes Moryson, in a note on 'The disposall of the whole Army in Ireland the seuen and twentieth of October 1601', lists all the horse and foot and their commanding officers 'Left at Loughfoyle', with the numbers of men under their charge, including under foot 'Captain *Gower*, 150'.[126] Moryson also alludes to a 'Captain *Goare*', and a 'Captain *Gore*', who may or may not be one and the same person.[127] When the Irish magnate Ruaidhrí Ó Domhnaill – named earl of Tyrconnell from 1603 – wrote to Lord Mountjoy on 1 November 1602 pleading his loyalty, it was 'Captain *Gore*' who was tasked with bringing him in.[128] This may be the Paul Gore who became a hugely influential Anglo-Irish figure and fathered a major dynasty.[129] Another Captain Gore is mentioned in an account of the failed Cadiz expedition of 1625:

> Public opinion was outraged not merely by the miscarriage
> of the Cadiz expedition, but by the acquittal of its comman-
> der, Lord Wimbledon, and his chief subordinates. 'The

---

[125] E. T. Bradley, 'Gower, Sir Thomas (*fl.* 1530–1577)', rev. Gervase Phillips, *ODNB*. Retrieved 23 July 2019. For a very Welsh Gower of an earlier period see Glanmor Williams, 'Gower, Henry (1277/8–1347)', *ODNB*. Retrieved 23 July 2019.

[126] Fynes Moryson, *An Itinerary* (London: 1617), p. 146.

[127] Moryson, *An Itinerary*, p. 105, p. 210. [128] Moryson, *An Itinerary*, p. 249.

[129] A. P. W. Malcomson, 'Belleisle and Its Owners', *Clogher Record* 16, 2 (1998): 7 (7–44).

> fault,' said a newsletter, 'is laid upon old Captain Gore, the
> only man who behaved himself well, and an old soldier of
> the Queen's.'[130]

The spelling of 'Gore' for 'Gower' may suggest its pronunciation, an especially loaded one in a military context as either a noun or verb.

The English Captain is, as the Welsh Captain observes, 'literatured in the Warres' (4.7.126), but military figures aside, perhaps the most renowned Gower for Shakespeare and his contemporaries on Bankside was John Gower (*c.* 1330–1408), the late medieval Romance poet considered second only to Chaucer in the English literary tradition. Shakespeare writes *Henry V* in 1599, possibly though not certainly the first play written for performance at the newly built Globe in Southwark. John Gower was a resident at the Priory of St Mary Overie in the same neighbourhood for the last forty or so years of his life. Upon his death, an ornate tomb was erected in his memory in the north aisle of the nave; an effigy of the poet rests upon the works that ensure his lasting fame: *Vox Clamantis*, *Speculum Meditantis*, and *Confessio Amantis*. After the Reformation, the priory at St Mary Overie was dissolved and the church was re-dedicated as St Saviour and is now better known as Southwark Cathedral. It was the local site of worship for those living on Bankside, and Shakespeare must have visited the space and seen Gower's tomb. This is also where Edmund Shakespeare, William's youngest brother, was interred.[131] Like his borrowings from Chaucer – another who knew Southwark well, beginning his *Canterbury Tales* in this neighbourhood – with *The Two Noble Kinsmen*, Shakespeare's late co-authored play with George Wilkins, *Pericles, Prince of Tyre*, features the character of Gower as a choric commentator. Since the Irish Captain appears in a scene with Scottish and Welsh soldiers of equal rank their voices arguably outweigh the 'English' voice of Gower.

[130] C. H. Firth, 'The Reign of Charles I', *Transactions of the Royal Historical Society* 6 (1912): 20 (19–64).

[131] See Stanley Wells, 'Shakespeare, Edmund (1580–1607)', in Michael Dobson and Stanley Wells, eds., *The Oxford Companion to Shakespeare*, 2nd ed., rev. Will Sharpe and Erin Sullivan (Oxford: Oxford University Press, 2001; 2015), p. 488.

The Scottish Captain

What of the quietest of the foursome, the peace-making Scottish Captain, who appears only in 3.3 and speaks a mere 0.4 per cent of the play's dialogue? According to James Bartley:

> Shakespeare's Captain Jamy . . . is rather taciturn and canny, compared with Macmorris and Fluellen, but although in this way he bears some resemblance to the conventional Scot of more recent years, he is an isolated case, and there is no further indication that these qualities were meant for Scottish. . . . Captain Jamy . . . show[s] differences from English in pronunciation only.[132]

What lies behind editorial decisions around national or regional characters and dialect? According to Noting that 'twenty-six of Jamy's fifty-two words are dialect forms', Vimala Pasupathi proposes that 'Characters with dialects . . . speak to the value of regional identities as commodities on stage and in print . . . whereas Shakespeare's Jamy in *Henry V* (1623) . . . suggest[s] their potential as a political liability'.[133] But this liability is also an opportunity to demonstrate loyalty: 'Whether [Jamy's] inclusion or exclusion in quartos of *Henry V* indicate deference to or criticism of James I, Shakespeare needs a Scottish Jamy to show Henry's ability to marshal the loyalties of "the weasel scot" away from his "auld alliance" with France to rally behind England'.[134]

Also noting differences between Q1 and the Folio text, Keith Brown set out to unyoke the two Celtic captains paired in much of the criticism:

> The 1600 Q text's omission of both Captain Jamy and Captain Macmorris has fostered a tendency among textual scholars to assume that the two soldiers are somehow bracketed together in the history of the composition of the play: that *both* must

---

[132] Bartley, 'The Development of a Stock Character II', p. 280.

[133] Vimala C. Pasupathi, 'Jockeying Jony: The Politics of Horse-Racing and Regional Identity in *The Humorous Magistrate*', *Early Theatre* 14, 2 (2011): 172, n.28; 145 (143–176).

[134] Pasupathi, 'Jockeying Jony', 151.

either have been dropped from the original text when this Q-version was put together, or jointly added to the play later. Thus the Oxford edition ... argues ... that both were cut in 1600: Macmorris as being less topical and amusing after Essex's return, and Jamy because he too (therefore?) was a comic character – a hostilely satiric figure who had to be cut to avoid further offence to the King of Scots.[135]

Brown fastens onto Jamy as a later addition, introduced to please James after his accession and that if you 'Delete Jamy's entrance, and all subsequent remarks by or to him, and III.3 runs perfectly smoothly'.[136]

We will return to Brown's claims about late additions, but what of historical Scottish captains? Where would one encounter such a figure, from an English perspective, other than at Boulogne or Berwick? The answer is Ulster. On 15 September 1584, Sir John Perrot, Lord Deputy of Ireland, wrote to the privy council about an encounter on the Antrim coast:

My self with the rest of the company are encamped before Dunluce ... situate upon a rock hanging over the sea, divided from the main with a broad deep rocky ditch ... and having no way to it but a small neck of the same rock ... It hath in it a strong ward, whereof the captain is a natural Scot, in who when I sent to summon them to yield, refused talk, and proudly answered (speaking very good English) that they were appointed and would keep it to the last man for the King of Scots' use: which made me to draw thither.[137]

Perrot's purpose was to 'banish the Scots and bring this province to that stay that it hath not been at any time heretofore'.[138]

---

[135] Brown, 'Historical Context and *Henry V*', *Cahiers Élisabéthains*, 29 (1986): 78–79 (77–81); emphasis in original.

[136] Brown, 'Historical Context and *Henry V*', 79; emphasis in original.

[137] David Edwards, ed., *Campaign Journals of the Elizabethan Irish Wars* (Dublin: Irish Manuscripts Commission, 2014), p. 167.

[138] Edwards, ed., *Campaign Journals*, p. 167.

Despite such glimpses of Scottish captains, Jamy remains an under-studied figure. The entry on Captain Jamy in *The Oxford Companion to Shakespeare*, for example, is disarmingly brief: 'He is a Scot in *Henry V* who has a conversation with *Fluellen and *MacMorris, 3.3'.[139] But recent work urges us to take the play's Scottish context more seriously. Lorna Hutson rejects the critical view 'that the insertion of "Captain Jamy" in a revised text of the play represents a compliment to James VI and I and an optimism about "Britain"'.[140] Gary Taylor, noting the absence of the four captains scene from the Quarto, remarked in his 1982 edition that:

> the gentle ridicule of Captain Jamy in 3.3 would hardly have recommended itself after 1603 (let alone before James himself, in 1605). Indeed it may not have recommended itself even in 1599; James, already the prime candidate as Elizabeth's successor, had made known his displeasure at certain dramatic representations of him and his countrymen.[141]

Yet to cast James in the role of censor is to miss his simultaneous importance as a patron of theatre. A single misconstrued source has fuelled much of the discussion around Jamy's supposed suppression. According to E. K. Chambers:

> In 1598 there were complaints in Scotland that 'the comedians of London should scorn the king and the people of this land in their play'. We do not know that these comedians were the

---

[139] Anne Button, 'Jamy, Captain', in Dobson and Wells, eds., *The Oxford Companion to Shakespeare*, p. 186. The Irish and Welsh captains do not fare much better in Button's other entries. MacMorris 'is an Irish officer who quarrels with *Fluellen, *Henry V* 3.3.' (p. 385); Fluellen is a Welshman who 'quarrels with *Macmorris [*sic*] (3.3), Williams (4.8), and Pistol (5.1)' (p. 123); and Gower 'is an English captain, friendly with Fluellen' (p. 148).

[140] Lorna Hutson, 'Forensic History: and Scotland', in Lorna M. Hutson, ed., *The Oxford Handbook of English Law and Literature, 1500–1700* (Oxford: Oxford University Press, 2017), p. 703 (pp. 687–708): 'Such an argument fails to take account of the strenuous ideological work performed by the play in effacing the idea of Scotland as a nation'.

[141] Taylor, ed., *Henry V*, pp. 15–16.

Chamberlain's men. The Scots are hardly treated in *Edward III*, printed in 1596, which may be theirs, and it is conceivable that the absence of the Captain Jamy episode (iii.2.69–153) from the 1600 quarto of *Henry V* may be due to censorship, although other explanations are also possible.[142]

Chambers later offers another possible solution to the supposed suppression of the four captains scene:

An alternative and perhaps more plausible conjecture is that the passage was censored in 1599, because of earlier offence given to James by theatrical references to Scotland. If so, we cannot suppose that it was restored when he saw the play on 7 January 1605 ... but the F printer may, quite properly, have ignored a deletion mark.[143]

Annabel Patterson took Gary Taylor to task for his suggestion that 'the Jamy and MacMorris episode ... was either "omitted to shorten the play or censored, because of King James's recently expressed irritation at dramatic ridicule of the Scots"'.[144] For Patterson, 'a cardinal rule governing the interpretation of textual divergences between quartos and folios' is 'that no single hypothesis is likely to be able to explain all the instances of textual divergence; and that it is better to admit this in advance than be forced to introduce exceptions that the primary hypothesis at its roots'.[145] James Shapiro sees the changing representation of the Scots in *Henry V* as bound up with historical cross-currents and contemporary politics:

With the King of Scots the leading contender to succeed Queen Elizabeth, Henry's warning that 'the Scot ... hath been still a giddy neighbour to us' (I, ii, 144–5) seems

[142] Chambers, *William Shakespeare: A Study of Facts and Problems*, p. 65.

[143] Chambers, *William Shakespeare: A Study of Facts and Problems*, pp. 392–393.

[144] Annabel Patterson, 'Back by Popular Demand: The Two Versions of *Henry V*', *Renaissance Drama* 19 (1988): 29–62, at 38.

[145] Patterson, 'Back by Popular Demand', 38–39.

uncharacteristically impolitic on Shakespeare's part. Many in the audience no doubt knew that Scottish mercenaries, fighting alongside the Irish, were awaiting Essex's forces in Ireland (even as anyone familiar with the chronicles upon which Shakespeare drew would have known that Scottish and Welsh forces fought alongside the French against Henry V while, confusingly, the Irish fought alongside Henry).[146]

John Kerrigan's analysis of the play's politics is equally subtle, detecting a shift from 'the weasel Scot' of the play's opening to a more favourable depiction:

> As the play moves forward, it leaves behind the legacy of medieval Anglo-Scottish antagonism and introduces Captain Jamy as a peacemaker among a group of Scottish, Irish, and Welsh officers who caricature, in their fractiousness, the difficulties that James VI would have to deal with when he came to power in England/Wales and Ireland. The irenic manner of Jamy the Scot has not been picked out by commentators, but audiences would have recognized it as one of James VI's most vaunted qualities. ... That the sequence involving the captains appears only in the 1623 Folio of Shakespeare's plays ... and is absent from a quarto (1600) which reflects early performance, suggests that it was never staged – a victim of the sensitivity of Anglo-Scottish and British-Irish relations during Elizabeth's declining years.[147]

Kerrigan's slashed Anglo-Welsh identity is characteristic of the latter's absorption ahead of Ireland and Scotland. Arguments persist over the reasons behind the absence of the four captains scene from the quarto. According to Thomas Berger: 'Neither Macmorris nor Jamy appears in the 1600 quarto ... due to

---

[146] James Shapiro, *1599: A Year in the Life of William Shakespeare* (New York: Harper Collins, 2005), p. 105.

[147] Kerrigan, *Archipelagic English*, p. 15.

abridgment, not problems of casting'.[148] Thus, according to this argument, the
scene's absence from the play's first printing is not as a performance issue but an
editorial one aimed at streamlining and strengthening the patriotic message.
Gary Taylor anticipated this argument in an earlier study:

> The Quarto's omission of the Jamy and MacMorris episode
> in 3.2 cannot be explained as a consequence of casting. Only
> three rather minor actors were available to play the parts,
> but there are few English actors who could not, at a pinch,
> passably imitate an Irish accent.[149]

Casting aside, national sensitivities continue to haunt the play in performance.
Reflecting on Nicholas Hytner's National Theatre production of *Henry V* in
2002–3, Sonia Massai noted that 'Robert Blythe and Tony Devlin played
Fluellen and Macmorris in their native Welsh and Northern Irish accents'
before going on to add:

> National stereotyping was downplayed by local editing of
> the text and by the excision of Jamy, which drastically
> reduced both the comic and the subversive potential often
> associated with these characters ... in all other respects,
> though, this production simply juxtaposed the higher rank-
> ing English characters, whose speech was normatively
> marked by prestige phonetic variations, to lower class and
> foreign characters, who were just as conventionally marked
> by lower status and put-on stage accents.[150]

The downplaying of the Scottish character is ironic give the weight attached
to name as an identification with the Scottish succession. Amanda

---

[148] Thomas L. Berger, 'Casting *Henry V*', *Shakespeare Studies* 20 (1988): 103n26
       (89–104).

[149] Gary Taylor, 'We Happy Few: The 1600 Abridgement', in Stanley Wells, ed.,
       Modernizing Shakespeare's Spelling, with Three Studies in the Text of Henry V
       (Oxford: Clarendon, 1979), p. 85 (pp. 72–119).

[150] Sonia Massai, *Shakespeare's Accents: Voicing Identity in Performance* (Cambridge:
       Cambridge University Press, 2020), p. 40.

Penlington's comments on this directorial decision to cut the Caledonian captain with the notable national forename are telling:

> The excision of Jamy was one tactic in avoiding national stereotyping but his removal from the play lessens the text's historical relevance. Editing the text (and especially editing out key moments) was at the heart of Hytner's approach to revising the character of Fluellen away from the comic tradition, so the leek scene (Act 5 scene 1) was cut.[151]

Names in Shakespeare are loaded by, among other things, his propensity for punning.[152] How loaded is that ostensibly Scottish name?[153] With the villainous Iago and Iachimo we know where we are, while with the invocations of Jacob in *Measure for Measure* and *The Merchant of Venice* we may be on more uncertain ground, but what of other instances of James? There is not a great deal to say about James Gurney (*King John*), Sir James Cromer (*2 Henry VI*), Sir James Tyrrel and Sir James Blunt (*Richard III*), or the fittingly named musician James Soundpost (*Romeo and Juliet*), although Biondello swearing by 'Saint Jamy' in *Taming of the Shrew* may be a loaded oath:[154]

> Nay, by S. *Iamy*,
> I hold you a penny,
> A horse and a man
> Is more then one,
> And yet not many. (7.71–75)

---

[151] Amanda Penlington, '"Not a Man from England": Assimilating the Exotic "Other" Through Performance, from Henry IV to Henry VI', in Willy Maley and Margaret Tudeau-Clayton, eds., *This England, That Shakespeare: New Angles on Englishness and the Bard*, (Ashgate: Burlington and Farnham, 2010), p. 171 (pp. 165–183).

[152] Patricia Parker, 'What's in a Name: And More', *SEDERI* 11 (2002): 101–149.

[153] See Andrew Gurr, 'Why Captain Jamy in *Henry V*', *Archiv für das Studium der Neueren Sprachen und Literaturen* 226, 2 (1989): 365–373.

[154] This Jamy is noted alongside the Scots captain in Francis Griffin Stokes, *A Dictionary of the Characters & Proper Names in the Works of Shakespeare* (London: G. G. Harrap, 1924), p. 168.

The four captains have indeed been seen as four saints:

> Shakespeare's use of four captains is complemented by his use
> of four saints who similarly stand for different constituencies.
> The play invokes St. David, the patron saint of Wales;
> St. Denis, the patron saint of France; St. George, the patron
> saint of England; and Sts. Crispin and Crispianus who, while
> not national patron saints like the other three, serve in the play
> as the general symbol of Henry's infantry army.[155]

Ian Brown notes that when Shakespeare has Jamy serve under Henry V he
does so 'improbably, of course, since in the Hundred Years War Scotland was
consistently an ally of France and many Scottish soldiers served the French
cause'.[156] It is worth remembering that the original James I (1394–1437), king
of Scots, was knighted by Henry V on St George's Day in 1421.[157] Andrew
Gurr comments thus on James I's service in France under Henry V:

> The presence of Captain Jamy with King Henry . . . is the more
> striking because Holinshed gives ample detail not just of
> a Scottish presence but of a James in Henry's army. And not
> just any Jamy, but King James I of Scotland. Henry in fact held
> James I captive for 18 years, from 1405, when James was only
> 11, to 1423, after Henry's death. After Agincourt Henry allowed
> him to go to France to fight as a private knight in the English
> army. He fought well against the dauphinists, notably at the
> siege of Dreux in 1421, which he helped Gloucester to win. He
> was the principal mourner at Henry's death at Bois in 1422.[158]

Gurr is rightly curious as to how a Scottish king – James I – fighting for an
English monarch against a French army that included many of his

---

[155] Alison A. Chapman, '*Henry V*'s Four Saints', in *Patrons and Patron Saints in
       Early Modern English Literature* (London: Routledge, 2013), p. 79 (pp. 79–85).
[156] Ian Brown, *Performing Scottishness: Enactment and National Identities* (Cham:
       Palgrave Macmillan, 2020), p. 67.
[157] M. H. Brown, 'James I (1394–1437)', *ODNB*. Retrieved 23 July 2019.
[158] Gurr, 'Why Captain Jamy', p. 370.

countrymen could be construed as a compliment to the second James I (James VI of Scotland).[159] The first James I was pressed into service – 'a captive and loyal servant of Henry V' – so unsurprisingly his subjects did not form an orderly queue to serve with him under the English crown.[160] Yet the Scots captain remains an anomaly in the scene, since 'no Scot other than King James served in Henry's army'.[161]

Gary Taylor has more recently argued that the Scottish captain is a 'plausible addition' rather than a cause for censorship for a Jacobean court performance, noting that adding 'Captain Jamy to the Elizabethan scene at Harfleur would have transformed it into an embodiment of James I's "Great Britain"'.[162] Lorna Hutson views the disappearing act that sees Scotland upstaged by Ireland and Wales in the histories through a different lens:

> The refusal of Shakespeare's *1 & 2 Henry IV* and *Henry V* even once to name the king of Scotland, James I (1406–1437), who was himself a poet, and who played an enforced role leading Henry's forces in France (inherently dramatic as a potential war crime), has made the kingdom itself seem to disappear from this period of English history. And if the bland and entirely dispensable part of 'Captain Jamy' was intended as an allusion to the real King James I, it has successfully compounded that effect.[163]

[159] Gurr, 'Why Captain Jamy', p. 371.

[160] Vimala C. Pasupathi, 'The Quality of Mercenaries: Contextualizing Shakespeare's Scots in *1 Henry IV* and *Henry V*', in Maley and Loughnane, eds., *Celtic Shakespeare*, p. 53 (pp. 35–60).

[161] Maurice Hunt, 'The "Breaches" of Shakespeare's *The Life of King Henry the Fifth*', *College Literature* 41, 4 (2014): 21n10 (7–24).

[162] Gary Taylor, 'One Book to Rule Them All: "The King James Version" of Shakespeare's Plays', *Shakespeare* (2023): 12; 14 (1–29) https://doi.org/10.1080/17450918.2023.2251940.

[163] Lorna Hutson, 'Scotland Un-kingdomed: English History on Stage', in *England's Insular Imagining: The Elizabethan Erasure of Scotland* (Cambridge: Cambridge University Press, 2023), p. 219 (pp. 188–219).

Gurr's claim that the Scottish captain and his Irish counterpart are the mercenaries of Henry's military camp is harder to accept, and Pasupathi cautions against the conflation of the two captains.[164] He is, rather, a conundrum who 'intervenes as a peace-maker amongst his fellow officers, but does so in ways that suggest his indifference to their conflict and England's as well'.[165]

Unlike Gower, whose identity is unproblematic, and unlike the touchy Irish captain and his patriotic Welsh interlocutor, Jamy is distinctive but does not declare his affiliation. As Froude observed: 'Captain Jamie never mentions Scotland: we learn his country from his dialect, and from what others say of him'.[166] Gary Taylor's note on Jamy reads: 'A common Scots name. The most famous living Scot was James VI, four years later to succeed Elizabeth, and already tipped as the prime candidate'.[167] We know that Captain Jamy was called James. Fluellen addresses him as 'good Captain James' (3.3.28).[168] But was James VI ever called Jamy? We know that James IV was called Jamy, chiefly by English commentators eager to disparage him. If we trace the name 'Jamy' through the sixteenth century we find it used in a particular way. Captain Jamy has been seen as a compliment to Elizabeth's successor, but if we look at English uses of the name from John Skelton's post-Flodden reference onwards, they are almost wholly uncomplimentary. 'The earliest extant printed ballad' is a satire on King James IV in the year of his death at Flodden.[169] Skelton's satire is addressed to 'Kynge Iamy'.[170] The typeface in the original which survives in a single copy in the British Library is somewhat illegible, but the 1545 reprint, entitled 'Skelton laureate against the Scottes', is clearer:

[164] Gurr, 'Why Captain Jamy', p. 370. Pasupathi, 'The Quality of Mercenaries', pp. 55–56.

[165] Pasupathi, 'The Quality of Mercenaries', p. 56.

[166] Froude, *The English in Ireland*, I, p. 8.   [167] Taylor, ed., *Henry V*, p. 165.

[168] Dutton, 'Methinks the Truth Should Live from Age to Age', p. 188.

[169] H. R. Plomer, *A Short History of English Printing, 1476–1898* (London: Kegan Paul, Trench, Trübner and Company, 1900), p. 47.

[170] John Skelton, *A ballade of the Scottysshe kynge* (London: 1513), p. 1.

> Kinge Iamy / Iemmy / Iocky my Io
> ye Summond our kyng / why dyd ye so
> To you / nothing it dyd accorde
> To Summon our kyng / your soueraygne lorde.[171]

The dedicatory verse by the printer Richard Grafton to Thomas duke of Norfolk in John Hardyng's *Chronicle* (1543) plays on the same scene of humiliation harped on by Skelton:

> The same your father, in the fyfth yere
> Of our moost noble kyng Henry the eyght
> When hys grace and his armie at Turney were
> And the same kyng Iamy, of Scotland streyght
> Agaynst England, his banner dyspleyght
> Vanquished the Scottes, & wt your helpyng hand
> Slew there king Iamy, and brought him to England.[172]

Further examples abound. In his discussion of the siege of Norham Castle in 1497 Edward Hall writes: 'Wherfore king Jamy thought yt to small purpose to tary any lenger in besegyng the castell, reysed his siege and returned into his awne realme'.[173] William Patten argues the clemency of Henry VIII after 'your last king Iamy with all your nobilitee had inuaded hys Realme' and asks 'what woold your owne kinge Iamy haue doon?'.[174] William Baldwin touches on the first James I: 'And to quicken vp your spirites, I wil take vpon me a tragicall person in deede, I meane kyng Iamy slayne by his seruauntes in his pryvy chamber, who although he be a Skot, yet seing he was brought vp in Englande where he learned the language, hys example also so notable, it were not meete he shoulde be forgotten'.[175] In his

[171] John Skelton, *Here after foloweth certayne bokes* (London: 1545?), B[r].

[172] John Hardyng, *The chronicle of Ihon Hardyng* (Londini: 1543), iiii[r].

[173] Edward Hall, *The vnion of the two noble and illustre famelies* (Londini: 1548), xliiii[r].

[174] William Patten, *The expedicion into Scotla[n]de of the most woorthely fortunate prince Edward* (London: 1548), biii[r], bv[r].

[175] William Baldwin, *A Myrroure for Magistrates* (London: 1559), xxxv[v]–xxxvi[r].

ventriloquist verse on James IV's daughter Margaret, John Phillips has her say 'king Iamy the fourth did soone decree,/ To enuy king Henry as well it is séene', following up with an account of her father's death at Flodden:

> My Uncle King Henry the eight of that name,
> Beholding of Iames, the surquedie and pride:
> Assembled his power this Prince for to tame,
> Whose folly a rod for him selfe did prouide.
> At Bramstome this battell should manly be tryde,
> In which as God would king Iamy was slaine,
> His Army dispersest and Skots put to paine.[176]

William Allen's allusion to 'the Scottish Heretiques from their lauful Soueraine' is glossed with a marginal note identifying the sovereign in question as '*Iamy*'.[177] Finally, perhaps the most remarkable instance of the name 'Jamy' referring – as all occurrences seem to do – to a Stuart king is in Philip Rosseter's 'Note and Tablature' for Thomas Campion's song, 'It fell on a sommers day', which appears to be an allegorical depiction of the projected Scottish succession with shades of Hal's borrowing of his father's crown in *2 Henry IV*:

> It fell on a sommers day while sweete Bessie sleeping laie
> In her bowre, on her bed, light with curtaines shadowed,
>   Jamy came shee him spies
> opning halfe her heauie eies.
> Jamy stole in through the dore,
> She lay slumbring as before,
> Softly to her he drew neere,
> She heard him, yet would not heare,
> Bessie vow'd not to speake,
>
>   . . .

---

[176] John Phillips, *A Commemoration [. . .] Margrit Duglasis* (London: 1578), Bii[v], Biii[r].

[177] William Allen, *A True, Sincere and Modest Defence, of English Catholiques* (Rouen: 1584), p. 5.

> She dreamp't not what he would doo,
> But still slept, while he smild
> To see loue by sleepe beguild.[178]

The 'Jamy' joke died hard. In a seventeenth-century broadsheet ballad Aphra Behn poked fun at Charles II's younger brother and the future James VII and II during the Exclusion Crisis, haunted by another Jamey, James Scott, Duke of Monmouth.[179] Scottish captains were resonant at a time when Wallace was being invoked as a counterweight to James. John Speed speaks 'of *Wallace*, whom his Countrey had once by common consent chosen for their defender, and *Captaine Generall*'.[180]

It is tempting to see Jamy as just another comic Celtic character, but like the myth of Scottish anti-theatricality the idea that the three non-English captains are there purely for comic effect is erroneous. Although it has been suggested that well into the seventeenth century, 'where a non-Shakespearean Scot does appear on the London stage during this period it is in the minor role of the comic servant', plays like *The Valiant Scot* give the lie to this generalization.[181] Later Scottish captains were less comfortable with their English counterparts. During Cromwell's Scottish campaign, on 13 September 1650, it was reported 'That a *Scots* Captain taken Prisoner, told the English Officers, *That their Ministers advised them, if they were taken, they should throw away their Bibles, for if the* English *took any with Bibles, they should have no Quarter*'.[182]

The Irish Captain

If Henry V knighting James I in the field in France disrupts our acquired sense of chronology the archipelagic plot thickens when we consider that

---

[178] Philip Rosseter, *A booke of ayres, set foorth to be song to the lute, orpherian, and base viol* (London: 1601), Song VIII (unpaginated).

[179] Aphra Behn, *A Most Excellent New Ballad: [. . .] Called Young Jamey* (London: 1681?).

[180] John Speed, *The Theatre of the Empire of Great Britaine* (London: 1612), p. 550.

[181] Adrienne Scullion, '"Forget *Scotland*": Plays by Scots on the London Stage, 1667–1715', *Comparative Drama* 31.1 (1997): 105 (105–128).

[182] Bulstrode Whitlocke, *Memorials of the English Affairs* (London: 1682), p. 456.

Figure 1 Richard II knights Henry of Monmouth (the future Henry V) in Ireland near Kilkenny 1399., Jehan Creton, *La Prinse et mort du roy Richart*, BL Ms Harley 1319, f5r. Reproduced by kind permission of the British Library.

Richard II knighted the future Henry V in Ireland in 1399, prior to his deposition at the hands of Henry's father (see Figure 1). Indeed, when Richard returned to defend his kingly right, Henry was detained at Trim Castle on the banks of the River Boyne, an 'honourable hostage' in much the way he would later keep young James I in France.[183] Richard II was the last English monarch to enter Ireland until William III and James II & VII faced off at the Battle of the Boyne in 1690, but the earlier presence of the teenage Henry casts a different light on the scene and on competing

[183] C. T. Allmand, 'Henry V (1386–1422)', *ODNB*. Retrieved 9 October 2023.

claimants to the crown (since young Monmouth was knighted while his father was aiming to dethrone Richard).

Charles Molloy's *The Half-Pay Officers* (1720) presents a couple of familiar figures:

> Brother Officers, *Fluellin* and *Mac Morris*; they seem very earnest, but 'tis upon the old Subjects of Discipline, Battles, and Sieges: And tho the Peace should last fifty Years, they'll talk of nothing but War.[184]

One place where the theatre of war persisted through what was otherwise categorized as peacetime was Ireland, and the vexed nature of the Irish conflict at the turn of the seventeenth century has been suggested as a reason for the omission of the Irish captain from the quarto.[185] It is this character's name that poses the most significant challenges. As one commentator notes: 'Though Shakespeare cannot be called the inventor of the stage Irishman, he created the first Irish soldier on the stage in Captain MacMorris'.[186] The character plays a role in studies of early modern nationality disproportionate to his role in *Henry V*. A marginal character in several senses, he appears in a single scene of the play, speaks a mere 205 words (0.8 per cent of the play's overall dialogue – most of which are in an argument that leads nowhere), before disappearing back into the war-torn French countryside. Yet despite his brief time onstage, he has made a lasting impact on criticism, and informed the broader perception and reception of the play. Amanda Penlington provides a guide to changing directorial practices in response to historical and political circumstances, but how far are these changes in performance reflected in editions of the play, and how accurate is their reading of the original context of the drama?[187] Indeed,

---

[184] Charles Molloy, *The Half-Pay Officers* (London: 1720), p. 10.

[185] Richard Dutton, *Shakespeare, Court Dramatist* (Oxford: Oxford University Press, 2016), p. 182.

[186] Annelise Truninger, *Paddy and the Paycock: A Study of the Stage Irishman from Shakespeare to O'Casey* (Bern: Francke, 1976), p. 26.

[187] Penlington, 'Not a Man from England', p. 171, citing James N. Loehlin, *Shakespeare in Performance: Henry V* (Manchester: Manchester University Press, 1996), p. 53.

how Irish is the Irish captain? What is his nation? According to Annelise Truninger, 'MacMorris speaks standard English, a mispronunciation being only slightly indicated. But a brogue is conveyed by the repetition of phrases and by the oaths, which Shakespeare apparently used a few years before Dekker'.[188]

We are often reminded that 'the most famous utterance in all of Stage Irishry belongs to the character Captain Macmorris in Shakespeare's *Henry V*'.[189] As Gary Taylor says, 'the problems of the British in Ireland have continued to lend his part the thrill of topical interest'.[190] In his note on the Irish captain Taylor remarks that 'Mac was notorious as a prefix for Irish names' and that 'The Irish were notorious as ferocious and bloodthirsty fighters'.[191] In a play about war and nationhood, the Irish captain, fighting as part of an English army against the French alongside fellow soldiers from Wales, Scotland, and, of course, England, twice poses a question that foregrounds issues of national identity: 'What ish my nation?' Indeed, the Irish Captain has the most usages of 'nation' in a single speech of any play, and in a play like *Henry V* that is especially significant. It was a question that resonated for audiences and playwrights. In *The Half-Pay Officers*, Molloy's Mac Morris declares:

> 'Ha, what ish my Nation? Ish my Nation a Villain and a Jack Sauce and a Rascal? – say what ish my Nation: As Crist shall save me, I will cut of your Head'.[192]

Shakespeare's Irish captain is a more complex figure. For Michael Neill, 'his inarticulacy on the topic of nationality is precisely Shakespeare's point'.[193] According to James Shapiro, 'What ish my Nation' is a four-word question left unanswered in *Henry V* that

---

[188] Truninger, *Paddy and the Paycock*, p. 27.

[189] Robert Moore, 'Overhearing Ireland: Mediatized Personae in Irish Accent Culture', *Language & Communication* 31, 3 (2011): 234 (229–242).

[190] Gary Taylor, ed. *Henry V*, p. 67. [191] Taylor, ed. *Henry V*, p. 165.

[192] Molloy, *The Half-Pay Officers*, p. 52.

[193] Michael Neill, 'Broken English and Broken Irish: Nation, Language, and the Optic of Power in Shakespeare's Histories', *Shakespeare Quarterly* 45, 1 (1994): 19n66 (1–32).

has generated more attention than perhaps any other in Shakespeare's plays besides Hamlet's 'To be or not to be?' Justifiably so, as those four words cut to the heart of Shakespeare and Irishness. And the question demands an answer.[194]

The five-word question that follows – 'Who talks of my Nation?' – is equally important. Dunbar Plunket Barton makes the useful point that Irish chiefs of clans were called '*capitanus nationis suæ*', and ventures: 'Is it not possible that, when *Captain Macmorrice* asks "What is my nation?" he had in mind the meaning which the word had for him as an Irish clansman?'

Barton lists several historical contenders as models for the Irish Captain and alludes to 'a map of Kerry dated 1597' that shows 'the MacMorrishes (*sic*) of Lixnaw … as a clan'.[195] Barton mentions in passing one 'David MacMorris', and he is an interesting case, or rather, they, since it looks like there were two David MacMorrises caught in the crossfire of conflicting allegiances in the period. In his account of the earl of Desmond's intrigues with Francis I in 1523, Richard Bagwell comments: 'The Earl and his seneschal David MacMorris were promised French pensions'.[196] A fuller account of the French King's commitment is given by James Hogan who cites a 'rough draft' of the treaty with Desmond:

> He shall give a pension to the Earl, and to David MacMorris, his master of the war (*senescallo guerrarum*). In return … the Earl shall levy war on the King of England, whilst the French army approaches the shores

[194] James Shapiro, 'What ish my nation? Shakespeare's Irish connections', *The Irish Times* (23 April 2016), www.irishtimes.com/culture/stage/what-ish-my-nation-shakespeare-s-irish-connections-1.2619173, accessed 4 June 2020.

[195] Duncan Plunket Barton, *Links between Ireland and Shakespeare* (Dublin and London: Maunsel, 1919), p. 121.

[196] Richard Bagwell, *Ireland under the Tudors, with a Succinct Account of the Earlier History*, Vol. 1 (London: Longmans, Green, 1885), p. 181.

of Ireland, with the view of driving Henry VIII. entirely
out of Ireland.[197]

The later David MacMorris alluded to by Barton treated with the English,
working alongside Richard MacMorris of the Brees in brokering a deal with
Sir Nicholas Malby, Governor of Connaught, in 1576.[198] These two
MacMorrises, caught between France and England, capture beautifully the
dilemma of Shakespeare's Irish captain. John Kerrigan, following in the
footsteps of Barton and others, cited a sample of Elizabethan Irish name-
sakes or near-name-sakes for Shakespeare's Irish captain and observed:
'Shakespeareans do not seem to have noticed and thought about these
MacMorrises'.[199] One early mention is by Gabriel Harvey in his *Letter-
Book* where he refers to 'an uncertayne autor in certayne cantions agaynst
the wylde Irishe, and namelye Mack Morrise'.[200] This 'Mack Morrise' is
most likely an allusion to James fitz Maurice Fitzgerald, who died in 1579.[201]

Despite the great variety of forms, Shakespeare's spelling of
'Mackmorrice' (like 'Fluellen') remains idiosyncratic and this prompts us
to reflect upon the extent to which the dramatist was knowingly anglicizing
an Irish name. The Irish prefix 'Mac' suggests otherwise. Is 'Mackmorrice',
like 'Fluellen', a strained phonetic spelling, or is the play on names more
subtle?[202] Like the Morris dance performed in Ireland by that 'wilde
Morisco' Jack Cade in *2 Henry VI* (9.365), the spikiness of Shakespeare's
Irish captain invites astonishment.[203] Music ties Pistol's song to the Morris

[197] James Hogan, *Ireland in the European System*, Vol. 1, 1500–1557 (London:
       Longmans, Green, 1920), p. 16.

[198] Barton, *Links between Ireland and Shakespeare*, p. 132.

[199] John Kerrigan, 'Oaths, Threats and *Henry V*', *The Review of English Studies* 63,
       261 (2012): 569 (551–571).

[200] *Letter-Book of Gabriel Harvey, A.D. 1573–1580*, ed. Edward John Long Scott
       (London: Camden Society, 1884), p. 100.

[201] Kerrigan, 'Oaths, Threats and *Henry V*', 569n63.

[202] Rory Loughnane, ed. *Henry V*, New Oxford Shakespeare: *Critical Reference
       Edition*, Vol. II, p. 2304.

[203] See Alan Brissenden, 'Shakespeare and the Morris', *The Review of English
       Studies* 30, 117 (1979): 1–11.

dance and to an Anglo-Irish cultural crossover from the mid sixteenth century. Studies of Shakespeare's use of Irish music suggests this was part of both popular and courtly culture at the time.[204] There was a performance culture at Kilkenny from John Bale's time in 1552, focused on passion plays and other activities: "An entry for 23 July 1610 apparently recorded the payment of 20 shillings: 'for keeping the apparel used on Corpus Christi day station, and the apparel of the morries and players of the Resurrection'".[205] We know of at least one exact contemporary 'kinsman' of Shakespeare's Irish captain who was a comic performer with a French connection and, allegedly, was a 'knave'. On 2 February 1598 William Paule wrote to Sir Robert Cecil: 'ffor Thomas mc Morris entituled a Baron from the Curte of Spaine His the verie same shaghaird knaue that was in England, & followed the frenche king in Sir Henry Untons tyme, in the nature of a Iester, & willyam mc Morris Is his elder brother'.[206] Fletcher's note reads: 'Nothing seems known about Thomas Mac Morris or his brother William, but evidently Thomas had attached himself to the French king as a (professional) fool'.[207]

There are other earlier and later historical figures of that name. Lawyer and satirist Edward Hake alludes to a certain '*Mack Morice*' in a work dedicated to the earl of Leicester:

> And how that *Stukeley* lost his life,
> among *Barbariens* late,
> A Marquesse of the *Romish* marke,
> O too vntimely fate:
> His part (alas) was yet to play

---

[204] For a detailed discussion see William Henry Grattan Flood, 'Shakespeare and Irish Music', in *A History of Irish Music*, 4th ed. (Dublin, Belfast, Cork, Waterford: Browne and Nolan, 1927), pp. 168–180.

[205] John Fry and Alan J. Fletcher, 'The Kilkenny Morries, 1610', *Folk Music Journal* 6, 3 (1992): 381 (381–383).

[206] PRO: SP 63/202/Part 1, f. 128, cited in Alan J. Fletcher, *Drama and the Performing Arts in Pre-Cromwellian Ireland: Sources and Documents from the Earliest Times until c.1642* (Cambridge: D. S. Brewer, 2001), p. 183.

[207] Fletcher, *Drama and the Performing Arts in Pre-Cromwellian Ireland*, p. 515n119.

in places neerer hande.
He ment and bent his forces he,
against the *Irish* landes
But what this Marquesse left vndone,
Mack Morice he contryvd:
And hotly gan pursue the charge,
But ah, it neuer thryuv'd.
For Martyrlyke, he lost his head,
a losse (in deede) to wayle:
Sithe holy Father, through this losse,
of his intent dooth fayle.[208]

John Derricke's *Image of Irelande* (1581; see Figure 2) flags the problematic nature for the New English of the prefixes 'Mac' and 'O':

Let this a lesson bee,
to this Rebellyng route:
To Macke, and O. to Rorie Ogge,
to all the Traitours stoute.[209]

Reducing Irish names to their prefixes was a way of attacking extended kinship networks that undermined English rule:

Who so did taste, once of that Sugred life,
And reape the fruite, that spryngeth of the same,
Bi't wildest Karne, b'it infant child or wife:
Wearte fearcest foe, by conquest worthie fame,
Weart Macke, or O. Macke deuil weart by name
I thinke if grace, did them conduct a right.
Theilde no exchange, though change at will thei might.[210]

---

[208] Edward Hake, *Newes out of Powles Churchyarde* (London: 1579), p. Fiii^v. For this to be news, this 'Mack Morris' must be James fitz Maurice Fitzgerald, who died in 1579. Anthony M. McCormack, 'Fitzgerald, James fitz Maurice (d. 1579)', *ODNB*. Retrieved 25 July 2019.

[209] John Derricke, *The Image of Irelande* (London: 1581), Giii^v.

[210] Derricke, *The Image of Irelande*, Ki^v.

Figure 2 'Rorie Oge O'More', John Derricke's Image of Ireland (1581). Reproduced by kind permission of the University of Edinburgh, De.3.76.

In Holinshed's *Chronicles* (1586), a list of 'The lords temporall, as well English as *Irish, which inhabit the countrie* of Ireland' includes 'Mac Maurice, *aliâs* Fitzgerald, baron of Kerie'.[211] In his allegorical Irish dialogue, *Solon His Follie* (1594), Richard Becon speaks of exactions laid on the Irish by their lords, 'and such did *Mac Morris* sometimes yeelde vnto the late Earle of *Desmond* attainted'.[212]

One historical figure from the period of the play's setting offers a fascinating sidelight on the Celtiberian border-crossing nature of military adventuring in the period. Janico Dartasso, 'born in Navarre, of Basque descent', found his way via Cherbourg, an Anglo-Navarrese garrison, to service under Henry Hotspur, with whom he was captured by the Scots in

---

[211] Raphael Holinshed, *The Second Volume of Chronicles: Conteining the Description, Conquest, Inhabitation, and Troblesome Estate of Ireland* (London: 1587), p. 38.

[212] Richard Becon, *Solon his follie, or a politique discourse, touching the reformation of common-weales conquered, declined or corrupted* (Oxford: 1594), p. 83.

1388. Thereafter Dartasso married 'an Anglo-Irish heiress, Joan Rowe, *née* Taafe', and acquired considerable property in Ireland. At this point, his biography begins to resemble Shakespeare's Irish captain. Serving variously as 'constable of Dublin, deputy to the king's admiral in Ireland and ... steward of Ulster', he followed Henry V to Harfleur.[213] A notable captain with an Irish connection from the period of the play's composition is Thomas Stukeley, the subject of two Elizabethan dramas, George Peele's *The Battle of Alcazar* (1588) and (Heywood's?) *The Famous History of the Life and Death of Captain Thomas Stukeley* (1596).[214]

Edmund Campion's treatise about Ireland from 1571 is printed in Sir James Ware's *Two histories of Ireland* (1633) where, under 'The temporall Nobility' we find 'Mac Morice alias Fitz Gerald, Baron of Kerye'.[215] This is intriguing since Elizabeth's Irish secretary Geoffrey Fenton urged the earl of Leicester to confer upon his nephew, Philip Sidney, the title of 'Baron of Kerry'. Fenton's proposal that Philip be made Baron of Kerry would have turned Sidney into the heir to a 'Mac Morice'.[216] Edward Denny, friend of Philip Sidney, was granted the land of Gerald Fitz Gerald, the 'rebel' earl of Desmond, in Tralee in Kerry. In 1550 Fitz Gerald married Joan (*d*. 1565), the daughter and sole heir of James fitz Maurice Fitzgerald, tenth earl of Desmond, thus becoming son-in-law of fitz-Maurice, that is, mac Maurice/mac Morris, so that Denny became an heir of sorts of Gerald mac(-in-law) Maurice.[217] In Spenser's *A View of the State of Ireland*, written around 1596 but first published 1633, Irenius decries those Old English settlers who 'are degenerate ... and ... have

---

[213] Simon Walker, 'Dartasso, Janico (*d.* 1426)', *ODNB*. Retrieved 23 July 2019.

[214] See Joseph Candido, 'Captain Thomas Stukeley: The Man, the Theatrical Record, and the Origins of Tudor "Biographical" Drama', *Anglia-Zeitschrift für Englische Philologie* 105 (1987): 50–68; Brian C. Lockey, 'Elizabethan Cosmopolitan: Captain Thomas Stukeley in the Court of Dom Sebastian', *English Literary Renaissance* 40, 1 (2010): 3–32.

[215] James Ware, *Two Histories of Ireland* (Dublin and London: 1633), p. 7.

[216] Michael MacCarthy-Morrogh, *The Munster Plantation: English Migration to Southern Ireland, 1583–1641* (Oxford: Clarendon Press, 1986), p. 26.

[217] We are grateful to Thomas Herron for this last point.

quite shaken off their *English* names, and put on *Irish* that they might bee altogether *Irish*'. Irenius elaborates thus: 'the *Mac-mahons* in the north, were aunciently English ... descended from the *Fitz Ursulas*, ... Likewise ... the *Mac-swynes*, now in *Ulster*, were aunciently of the *Veres* in *England*, but ... for hatred of English, so disguised their names'.[218] Since Spenser urged the abolition of the surname prefix 'Mac' in *A View* it is unsurprising that Shakespeare's Irish captain should be so touchy.[219]

One of Essex's predecessors as Elizabeth's Irish viceroy, Sir William Russell, records in his 'Journal of all Passages' for Monday 14th April 1595 the execution of 'Edmund McMorris'.[220] Another MacMorris, contemporaneous with Shakespeare's play, crops up in a passage on events in Ireland in April 1603 in Richard Cox's *History of Ireland* (1689–90), where we learn that 'Sir *Charles Willmot* (who was besieging *Mac-Morris* in *Ballingary* Castle) immediately repair'd to *Cork*'.[221] Perhaps the most intriguing of these contemporary figures is Pádraigín Mac Muiris (*c.* 1551–1600), Lord Kerry, Irish-born, English-raised, who spent the first twenty years of his life at the court of Mary and Elizabeth while his father served the Duke of Milan.[222] Celebrated in a Gaelic poem of the 1590s, he was mooted a century ago as a possible prototype for Shakespeare's Irish captain.[223] Part of the Munster Rebellion that overthrew Spenser's estate, he died in 1600. Patricia

[218] Ware, *Two Histories of Ireland*, pp. 45–46.

[219] Edmund Spenser, *A View of the State of Ireland*, in Ware, ed., *Two Histories*, p. 109.

[220] Cited in Edwards, ed., *Campaign Journals of the Elizabethan Irish Wars*, p. 211.

[221] Richard Cox, *Hibernia Anglicana*, 2 Vols. (London: H. Clark for Joseph Watts, 1689–1690), I, p. 4.

[222] Christopher Maginn, 'Fitzmaurice, Patrick, seventeenth baron of Kerry and Lixnaw (*c.*1551–1600)', *ODNB*. Retrieved 22 October 2023.

[223] Osborn Bergin, 'A Poem by Domhnall Mac Dáire', *Ériu* 9 (1921/1923): 160–174. Bergin remarks that while 'the name might easily have reached Shakespeare's ear [...] A medley of national characteristics, real or imaginary, a little broken English, and a good Irish name' were enough to prompt the playwright without individual models (161). The poem is discussed in Patricia Palmer, 'Missing Bodies, Absent Bards: Spenser, Shakespeare and

Palmer rehearses contemporary candidates for Shakespeare's Irish captain with the aim not of locating 'the "real" MacMorris, but trying to use writings associated with these historical figures to move into that other culture from which one side of the dialogue we want must come':

> MacMorris or Mac Muiris is the gaelicized form of the Anglo-Norman name, FitzMaurice. The shift from Fitz to Mac testifies to the Hibernicization of that clan, a process almost inevitable given their long tenure in the southwest, far from the influence of the English Pale.[224]

Sir John Davies links MacMorris with an Old English tendency to 'not only forget the English Language . . . but . . . bee ashamed of their very English Names . . . One was called *Mac Morice* chiefe of the house of Lixnaw; . . . And this they did in contempt and hatred of the English Name and Nation'.[225]

A short description of Connaught published in 1615 includes among 'men of greatest note and reputation in this countie . . . *Mac Morris*'.[226] In his account of the events of 1603 Fynes Moryson observes: 'Sir *Charles Wilmott* Gouernour of *Kerry* . . . had before the siege of *Dunboy* prosecuted *Mac Morris*, cleered *Kerry* of all Rebels, and prosecuted them into *Desmond*'.[227] Charting Sir John Perrot's progress through Ireland in the 1580s and his encounter with the earl of Ormond, a seventeenth-century commentator

---

a Crisis in Criticism', *English Literary Renaissance* 36, 3 (2006): 387–389 (376–395).

[224] Palmer, 'Missing Bodies, Absent Bards', p. 385.

[225] John Davies, *A discouerie of the true causes why Ireland was neuer entirely subdued* (London: 1612), pp. 182–183.

[226] Pierre d'Avity, sieur de Montmartin, *The estates, empires, & principallities of the world* (London: 1615), p. 30.

[227] Moryson, *An Itinerary*, p. 273. This is followed by a reference to '*Mac Morris*, being daily assaulted by the English', and English actions in the south-west of Ireland entail 'leauing no Rebell in *Mounster* but *Mac Morris* [. . .] whereof *Mac Morris* in few daies was well beaten and spoiled of all he had by *Sir Char. Wilmott*' (p. 274).

remarks: 'This Earle first met him in *Connaught* with *Mac Morris* . . . and certaine Septs of the *Galloglasses*, who accompanied him to *Limbrick*'.[228] If the Old English in Ireland, the descendants of the twelfth-century settlement, had aliases or nicknames then so too did their lands. Thomas Stafford's *Pacata Hibernia* (1633) prints 'A Letter from the Mounster Rebels' dated 24 June 1600 that begins: 'All heartie Commendations from *Mac Maurice*, and the rest undernamed'.[229] In 1669 'An Act for strengthning of Letters Patents past and to be past, upon any of His Majesties Commissions of Grace for the Remedy of defective Titles' included a claim by the crown to 'all the several Territories, precincts of Land and Countries commonly known or called by the name or names of . . . Kilecoolenelin, alias Coolenelem, alias Mac Morris his Country'.[230] The crown's claim on the country of Mac Morris recalls the predicament of Shakespeare's captain, but also those sixteenth-century historical MacMorrises who found themselves skewered between French – and Spanish – allegiances and an expansive Englishness yoked to Welsh and later Scottish coadjutants. According to Thomas Tracy:

> The four captains are recalled in Jonson's *Bartholomew Fair* by the characters Knockem, Whit, Haggis, and Bristle. Haggis and Bristle are Scottish and Welsh members of the Watch who patrol the fair, and Captain Whit is their stage-Irish informer. The English Captain Knockem, although not officially connected to the Watch, has a close relationship with Whit—together they procure prostitutes for the fairgoers.[231]

In this section, we have mined and countermined the early modern period in search of precedents, antecedents, and contemporary analogues for the

---

[228] E. C. S. , *The gouernment of Ireland vnder [. . .] Sir Iohn Perrot* (London: 1626), p. 14.

[229] Thomas Stafford, *Pacata Hibernia* (London: 1633), p. 58.

[230] *Anno Regni Caroli Regis Angliae, Scotiae, Franciae & Hiberniae Decimo quinto* (Dublin: 1669), B1[r].

[231] Thomas Tracy, 'Order, Authority, Shakespearean History, and Jonsonian Comedy', *Ben Jonson Journal* 11,1 (2004): 111 (103–119).

names of the four captains. Our aim has been to address the four captains individually while demonstrating the extent to which such compartmentalization inevitably overlooks the intertwined relationships that make absolute distinctions impossible. In doing so we have moved from a Celtic to an archipelagic perspective. In the next section, we turn to the editorial and critical concomitants of the use of certain forms of names for these characters.

4 Four Captains

The four captains appear together for a single scene on a single page in the First Folio version of *Henry V* (see Figure 3). This 1623 version is the primary copy text for all modern editions of the play rather than the 1600 quarto. It is a curiously irregular text, likely based upon Shakespeare's autograph papers or a transcription of them.[232] An editor, working through the Folio text and past editions, might be first struck by the large number of errors in the text, not least given the significant challenges posed by the play's frequent use of the French language (most notably, 3.4 [scene 13] consists of an English language lesson in French) and the irregularly introduced phonetic representations of regional dialect.[233] An editor might be struck also by just how international the play seems, jumping setting between various named places in England and France, and introducing characters from France and the four countries of the Atlantic Archipelago. There are stereotypes introduced about French pride, Welsh leeks, and Irish hot-headedness. It is a play then that in its very fabric calls attention to regional differences in terms of language, speech, customs, and characteristics. But even though the play flags its internationalism it is also, and conspicuously, an anglicized

---

[232] William Shakespeare, The four captains scene is not present in the early alternative version of the play, *The Cronicle History of Henry the Fift* (London, 1600).

[233] See 'Introduction' to Rory Loughnane, ed. Henry V, in *New Oxford Shakespeare: Critical Reference Edition*, Vol. 2 (Oxford: Oxford University Press, 2017), pp. 2301–2306.

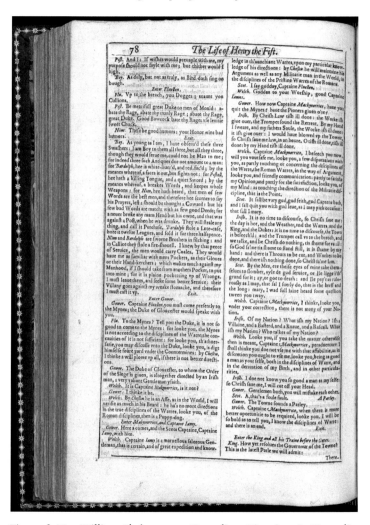

Figure 3 Mr. William Shakespeares Comedies, Histories, & Tragedies (London: 1623), h5v. Reproduced by kind permission of the Harry Ransom Center, Carl H. Pforzheimer Library, -q- PFORZ 905 PFZ.

version of internationalism. In this English play, written for primarily English audiences, the representation of international differences is viewed through an English lens.

How might an editor usefully negotiate the play's anglicized form of internationalism? They might begin by preparing a list of characters which will then provide the template for how these characters are identified in stage directions and speech prefixes. The first challenge is the names assigned to the large number of French characters. Should their names be translated into French or retained as weak English transliterations? In seeking consistency, the editor will have a difficult initial choice to make: whether to modernize non-anglophone words to their modern current form or to modernize, in effect, the transliteration included in their control text. So, should 'Grandpree' be 'Grandpré'? Or 'Orleans' be 'Orléans'? Or 'Mountjoy' be 'Montjoye'? Should the French heir apparent be the 'Dolphin', consistently used throughout the Folio text, or the 'Dauphin'? What, an editor might ask, would be the point in retaining the weak transliterations when the correct French form is readily available? But, in the case of 'Dolphin', does this delete contemporary playful usage?[234]

Let us consider 'Mountjoy/Montjoye', briefly, in this respect. Charles Blount, Lord Mountjoy, succeeded Essex in Ireland. Henry addresses this French Herald in a manner which seems particularly loaded (and is present in both Q and F):

> and so *Mountioy*, *fare you well.*
> The summe of all our Answer is but this:
> We would not seeke a Battaile as we are,
> Nor as we are, we say we will not shun it:
> So tell your Master. (3.6.137–141)

---

[234] For such punning on the lively aquatic mammal, see, for example, Joshua Sylvester, *The Parliament of vertues Royal* (London: 1614), B1^r-^{v}; see also 'His delights/ Were Dolphin-like' in Terri Bourus, ed., Antony and Cleopatra in *New Oxford Shakespeare: Critical Reference Edition*, Vol. 2 (Oxford: Oxford University Press, 2017).

Henry expressly asks for the French herald's name and is given the answer, 'Mountioy' (3.6.113). In his note on these lines Dover Wilson remarks: 'Montjoy is not a name, as Sh. implies, but the title of the chief herald of France (in fact, a 'quality'), borrowed from 'Montjoy St Denis!' the French K.'s war-cry'.[235] According to Richard Dutton, the French Herald was not intended to namecheck the future lord deputy of Ireland, since 'Mountjoy had no part in the 1599 Irish expedition'.[236] For Dutton the coincidence of 'Montjoy/Mountjoy' was 'unforeseeable in 1599 but unmissable in 1602'.[237] Yet Mountjoy's name was linked with Ireland in November 1598, when he was nominated by the privy council for the lord deputyship. In the event, he was leapfrogged by Essex's appointment. Mountjoy finally accepted the post in November 1599 and left for Ireland in February 1600.[238] *Henry V* is a play preoccupied with names, including placenames, and has the joint highest allusions to names in the corpus.[239] Indeed, when Henry offers Montjoy 'my ioynts' (4.3.124) we may detect paranomasia. Our point here is that an editor who introduces modern French forms as a standard practice may actually erase a set of telling resonances introduced by Shakespeare and perceptible to alert auditors at early performances of the play;

[235] John Dover Wilson, ed., *King Henry V* (Cambridge: Cambridge University Press, 1947; 1968), p. 157.

[236] Dutton, 'Methinks the Truth', p. 201.

[237] Dutton, 'Methinks the Truth', p. 202.

[238] Christopher Maginn, 'Blount, Charles, eighth Baron Mountjoy and earl of Devonshire (1563–1606)', *ODNB*. Retrieved 21 June 2024.

[239] We might think also of Pistol's onomastic interest: '*Le Roy*? a Cornish Name: Art thou of Cornish Crew?' (4.1.51). See Cristina Paravano, '"Peden bras vidne whee bis cregas": Cornish on the Early Modern Stage', in Donatella Montini and Irene Ranzato, eds., *The Dialects of British English in Fictional Texts* (London: Routledge, 2021), pp. 91–107: 'Le Roi clearly denotes a mispronunciation of the French "le roi", and can't be related to Cornish. The claim of Cornish origin for the king, who was actually born in Monmouth, Wales, may allude to a now-lost play entitled *Harry of Cornwall*, performed around 1592 by Lord Strange's Men' (p. 94).

that is, in committing to a policy of internationalism, might an editor risk also losing provincialism?

Of course, it still makes good sense that French characters in the play would pronounce any French names correctly. But what of this exchange in 4.7 (scene 24):

Kin. [. . .]
       What is this Castle call'd that stands hard by.
Her. They call it *Agincourt.*
King. Then call we this the field of *Agincourt*, (4.7.75–77)

The French herald would presumably use the French pronunciation of 'Azincourt' but would the King, who it is later implied has little French?[240] And, for an English audience, who grew up learning about Henry V's victory at Agincourt, would there be a perceptible difference between the way the French herald and the King say the word? There is nothing in the herald's dialogue to suggest he speaks in a specifically 'French' way, but should that be signified for readers in the text? Was Shakespeare, in writing 'Agincourt', knowingly adopting an English trans-literative version of the French town's name, or attempting to reproduce an unknown French spelling? Is the editorial onus to preserve authorial idiosyncrasy and inconsistency or to modernize and regularize in a consistent way that renders the text intelligible to a modern international readership? Whatever the editorial choice, 'Agincourt' or 'Azincourt', it will have concomitant editorial and critical implications for other non-Anglophone words in the edition which should at least be considered if made on an ad hoc basis. If seeking consistency, the choice will have knock-on effects for the modernizing treatment of placenames like 'Britaine', an

---

[240] See Henry's struggles in communicating in French at 5, 2.163–168; a less charitable reading of the character might interpret this as Henry's strategic powerplay to force Katherine to speak his language, a tactical procedure of many invaders. The historical Henry would been Francophone, so even introducing such apparent struggles might be read as a post-Reformation Anglocentric erasure of an Anglo-Norman/Anglo-French historical reality.

anglicized version of 'Bretagne', and proper names such as 'Mountjoy', 'Orleans', and 'Grand Pre', of which the modern French forms are 'Montjoye', 'Orléans', and 'Grandpré'. The play is notably inconsistent in its use of French: when together, French characters speak to each other at times in standard English (e.g., 2.4 [scene 8]) and other times almost entirely in French (e.g., 3.4 [scene 13]); and when encountering English-speaking characters, French characters speak at times in standard English (e.g., 3.6 [scene 15]) and other times entirely in French (e.g., 4.4 [scene 21]). This is entirely unproblematic in performance, but it does signal some of the difficulties for editors in attempting to apply measures consistently.

The names of the four captains pose even more significant onomastic challenges for an editor. In the Folio text of 3.3 (scene 12), three of the four captains are identified by their personal names in their entrance stage directions but by their nationalities in speech prefixes. Thus, '*Makmorrice*' in stage direction is '*Irish*' in speech prefix, '*Fluellen*' is '*Welch*', and '*Iamy*' is '*Scot*'. Only the Englishman, '*Gower*' remains '*Gower*'. This is the only use of '*Welch*' for the Welsh captain, and an editor adopting either the *first used* or *most-often used* rule for speech prefixes, would feel compelled to change these in a regularized modern edition to whatever proper name they have given this character. Similarly adopting either of these rules, an editor should then adopt '*Irish*' and '*Scot*' for the Irish and Scottish captains; they only appear in this scene and only have this designator in speech prefix. But these simple adoptions would create the anomalous situation whereby the Irish and Scottish characters are identified by nationality while the English and Welsh are accorded proper names. So, an editor, and as all editors have done since Rowe, might feel compelled to introduce proper names in speech prefixes for the Irish and Scottish characters, creating a parity across treatment of the characters. But does this practice of regularization actually blind readers to the political game that Shakespeare introduces here, which he compounds with their subsequent discussion of nationhood? Is it not significant that the Welsh Captain is identified by his national marker, where elsewhere he is not, while in the company of the Scot and Irishman? Is it not significant that the Englishman alone evades the national identifier? Or is that national identifier assumed? Following in the tradition of Rowe, any editor producing a regularized modern-spelling edition of *Henry V* will seek to be consistent. But how does such consistency serve the reader's understanding? Let us dig a little deeper.

The other editorial choice, how to identify these characters' proper names, is even more overtly political. *Henry V* fixates on cultural differences of language and conduct. In this context, names and naming are politically charged, and not only for the four captains. Across the Folio text of *Henry V*, the Welsh Captain is primarily designated by versions of '*Fluellen*' in stage directions, speech prefixes, and dialogue. Editors since Rowe have thereby felt little hesitation in using the name 'Fluellen' (or versions of it) as the regular, modernized form in all instances, and introducing it where variants occur. In 3.3 (scene 12), however, when in the company of the other three captains, there is a sudden outcropping of the speech prefix '*Welch*' for this character. This aligns and coincides with the speech prefix identification of the Irish captain as '*Irish*' and the Scottish captain as '*Scot*'. Of the four captains, only the Englishman Gower is designated by name and not by nationality ('*Gower*'). In modern editions of the play, this distinction is either lost entirely or diminished. And there is strong editorial logic for sticking with the Welsh Captain's proper name. The captains from Ireland and Scotland appear in only this scene, while the Welsh Captain has been some version of '*Fluellen*' in stage directions and speech prefixes from the beginning. So, if an editor sought the nationalistic flavour of the speech prefixes in 3.3, they would have to change all of the earlier and later speech prefixes for this character to '*Welsh*'. But, as names given in stage directions must align consistently with speech prefixes, they would then also have to introduce '[*Welsh*]', in some way, to the entrance directions for this character. It would also create the anomalous situation whereby '*Welsh*' is inhabiting a stage, where all the other characters are identified by name (e.g., '*Bates*'), nickname (e.g., '*Pistol*'), or title (e.g., [Archbishop of] '*Canterbury*'). So, '*Welsh*' may be ruled out, and we will discuss its concomitant critical effect next, but what proper name is in?

Andrew Gurr's approach to naming in his 1992 edition of the play was most notable for his treatment of the Welsh captain: 'The Shakespearean spelling of his name, which *F* renders as "Fluellen" and which *Q* makes into

"Flewellen", is phonetically very close to the modern "Llewellyn", which must therefore be the appropriate form to use in a modernised-spelling edition'.[241] The critical reception of Gurr's onomastic innovation was cool. For Park Honan:

> Though Gurr has reasons for it, one hopes his change of Fluellen to 'Llewellyn' is a piece of built-in obsolescence. The Welsh captain's name is 'Fluellen' in the 1623 Folio, 'Flewellen' in the 1600 Quarto. A 'Fluellen' is listed as a recusant at Stratford with John Shakespeare, as the editor knows, and M. C. Andrews points to Gerard's *Herbal* (1597) with its remarks on the speedwell, which is 'in Welch … called Fluellen' and contrasts with the leek; see *Notes and Queries*, ccxxxi (1986), 354–6. Though Gurr is reasonable and provocative, his modernizing of 'Fluellen' perhaps leads to an associative loss.[242]

Claire McEachern was equally guarded:

> The most striking modernization, that of Fluellen's name – to Llewellyn – may, as Gurr notes in his introduction, be 'phonetically very close to the modern "Llewellyn", which must therefore be the appropriate form to use' (63); yet it seems, to this reader at least, overweening in its scrupulous-ness and oddly anachronistic in its denial of the play's received cultural location – especially given that Fluellen is a character more than likely to render even his own name unfamiliar in the turn of dialect.[243]

---

[241] Andrew Gurr, ed., *King Henry V* (Cambridge: Cambridge University Press, 1992), p. 63.

[242] Park Honan, 'Review: *King Henry V*', *Notes and Queries* 41, 4 (1994): 554 (553–554).

[243] Claire McEachern, 'Review: *King Henry V*', *Shakespeare Quarterly* 45, 4 (1994): 488 (485–489).

Such assessments, focusing on the anomalous nature of this single innovation, reveal a larger problem with Gurr's editorial approach. For while 'Fluellen' became 'Llewellyn' and 'Mountjoy' became 'Montjoy', 'Agincourt' and 'Grand Pre' remained the same. The problem was one of inconsistency with non-anglophone names.[244] Adopting 'Llewellyn' over 'Fluellen', given the paucity of evidence that this was anything but a weak transliteration of the familiar Welsh name, seems to us entirely valid and editorially sound. But Gurr committed to an internationalist principle by adopting 'Llewellyn' without sticking to it; he had his cake, or perhaps leek, and ate it too.

What of the other three Captains? The English Captain can only be 'Gower' by proper name. And unlike the Welsh Captain, when appearing elsewhere in the play, he retains the consistent speech prefix of some version of '*Gower*' throughout. Gower is a name with Saxon, Norman, Welsh and French roots, perhaps motley enough for an English captain? John Gower was said by Caxton to be Welsh. Williams is of course a Welsh name. Since Henry claims Welsh identity, you could say there are few English characters of note in the play.[245] But, editorially, there is no imperative to change '*Gower*' unless an editor seeks to introduce a radical approach to preserve the nationalistic flavour of 3.3, changing each of this character's speech prefixes to '*English*' and retaining '*Welsh*', '*Irish*', and '*Scot*' for the other Captains. But this would have the knock-on effect, as we have seen, of forcing an editor to change all the other speech prefixes and entrance directions for the Welsh Captain, and, even more significantly, it would

---

[244] Gary Taylor's 1982 edition has: 'Fluellen', 'Jamy', 'MacMorris', and 'Gower'; reprinted essentially in 1986 and 2005. Taylor's edition is otherwise more faithful to non-anglophone spelling but not always consistent: For example, he adopts 'Grandpré' as a character name but retains 'Agincourt' over 'Azincourt'.

[245] The ODNB entry clings to Gower's Englishness: 'There is nothing to support Caxton's assertion in his edition of Gower's long English poem, the *Confessio amantis* (1483), that Gower was "a squyer borne in Walys in the tyme of kyng Richard the second". This was perhaps suggested by the region of Gower in south Wales.' Douglas Gray, 'Gower, John (*d.* 1408), poet', *ODNB*. Retrieved 25 October 2023.

mean that when Gower appears in 4.7 and 4.8 as '*English*', when accompanied by other English soldier characters, such as Williams. Caught in this bind, the editor must, paradoxically, preserve Gower's proper name, while removing the Welsh Captain's national identifier. And, in doing so, they have discovered a situation whereby two of the four characters must be identified by their personal names, which has knock-on effects for the other two.

The case of the Scottish Captain's name is relatively straightforward. In his entrance direction, as noted, he is '*Captaine Iamy*', and twice before he meets the English and Welsh Captains he is described as '*Captaine Iamy*'. When the Welsh Captain addresses him, he calls him '*Captaine Iames*'. Is the shift from the shortened familiar version of '*Iamy*' to the complete '*Iames*' a mark of deferential respect? Perhaps, but who can tell? He is never addressed by name again. So, with four instances of '*Iamy*' to one of '*Iames*' (the Welsh Captain's 'good Captain James') an editor may feel compelled to choose the former. Adopting the proper name for a modern edition, the options are 'Jamey', 'Jamy', or 'Jamie'. The final option can probably be ruled out. The Welsh Captain's name can be either a personal name or a family name. But the Irish Captain's name can only be a family name. Gower is also a family name. It would be odd if Shakespeare chose to designate only one of the four captains by a personal name. So 'James' is more likely to be the Scottish Captain's family name and 'Jamey' or 'Jamy' a corruption of it. (The relevant passage is in prose so the number of syllables in the Scottish Captain's name is irrelevant for meter.) An editor might reasonably choose either, though 'Jamey' offers the easier modernized reading. But this means changing each of the consistently used speech prefixes of '*Scot*' to '*Jamey*'. The editorial logic for this is dictated by the residual effect of the decisions made with the speech prefixes for the Welsh and English Captains. Could an editor reasonably produce a scene, filled with nationalistic tension, in which two characters are assigned proper names in speech prefixes and two representative, if not reductive, national identifiers?

And so, to the Irish Captain. In the Folio text, the character is first introduced in a stage direction as '*Makmorrice*', his four speech prefixes read '*Irish*.' and the five times he is addressed in dialogue he is '*Mackmorrice*'. In

Rowe, as we have seen, this becomes regularized as 'Mackmorrice' in stage directions and dialogue with '*Mack*' for speech prefixes (curiously, however, he is 'Mackmorris' in Rowe's list of characters). In later editions, the more popular forms became 'MacMorris' or 'McMorris'. Not a large leap, one might think; it seems like regular editorial practice to go from 'Makmorrice' to a reader-friendly version of 'McMorris' or 'Macmorris'. As with most Anglo-Irish exchanges, however, the situation is considerably more complicated. As we have noted, the name is a Gaelicized surname based on the Anglo-Norman patronymic 'fitz Maurice'. To explain, the Christian name 'Mauritius' came into Irish through Anglo Norman as 'Muiris' (from an Anglo-Norman form 'Morice' or 'Moris' or some such). The Anglo-Normans at the time used patronymics rather than surnames so 'Morice fitz Gerald' was 'Maurice son of Gerald' and Maurice's son Gerald would be 'Gerald fitz Morice'. The Irish were already using hereditary fixed surnames (i.e., compare the English, James Peter's son is a patronymic, but James Peterson is a surname). The Anglo-Normans now copied the Irish surnames by making 'fitz (i.e., 'son of') Morice' a surname 'FitzMorice', and when they became Irish speaking they Gaelicized it as 'Mac Muiris' ('mac' meaning 'son of' in Gaelic). This is the regular spelling of that surname in Irish but when English clerks were trying to write Irish surnames (e.g., in the Fiants) they had great difficulty, whence the variety of spellings they use. Barton also points to the name having 'an Irish prefix and a Norman termination'.[246] (What ish my termination?)

If an editor has committed to using the Welsh Captain's proper name, retaining 'Gower' for the English Captain, and, because of these decisions, introducing the proper name for the Scottish Captain in that character's speech prefixes, then they are left with little choice about what to do with the Irish Captain: a proper name is required. But which one? The most commonly adopted forms, some version of 'Macmorris' or 'McMorris', are anglicized modernizations of the Irish name. If the editor has already ventured along an international path with names and naming, in this most international of Shakespeare's plays, and adopted the non-controversial 'Montjoye' for 'Mountjoy', then what is the editorial defence behind

---

[246] Barton, *Links between Ireland and Shakespeare*, p. 121.

adopting 'Macmorris' or 'McMorris'? Why would the little-heralded French Herald have a modern French form while the Irish Captain has a modern English form? If seeking consistency, if adopting forms like 'Llewellyn', 'Montjoye', 'Azincourt', and so on, the editor is compelled to introduce the modern Irish form of the name: 'Mac Muiris'.

Our scene fills out. The four captains, 'Llewellyn', 'Gower', 'Jamey', and 'Mac Muiris', meet near the battlefield, and an argument erupts. What have we gained or lost through the editorial process? Such naming would commit the overall edition to introducing modern non-anglophone words, where required. We have gained consistency, therefore, with each character identified by their personal name, modernized to reflect their national pedigree and highlighting the international nature of the exchange. So, too, no names in speech prefixes contradict others; that is, *Gower* does not clash with *Welsh*, *Irish*, and *Scot*. The consistency is appealing and less jarring. But, in a very real sense, *Gower* does encounter *Welsh*, *Irish*, and *Scot*, as established by the Folio text, and this is now invisible to the reader. This is one example from one play: what else has been lost in the early modern plays of Shakespeare and others through an editorial commitment to consistency?

Coda

Recent criticism has begun to move beyond the idea that the four captains – or at least three of them – are mere caricatures or national stereotypes.[247] But these archipelagic officers remain bound up with critical questions of identity and antipathy. Indeed, Shakespeare scholars have at times appeared complicit with the negative perceptions of the Celtic characters that they see themselves as merely commenting on. Consider, for example, Stephen

---

[247] There are still exceptions: 'Shakespeare's *Henry V* offers a famous example of heteroglossia in the scene in which Captain Fluellen the Welshman, Captain Macmorris the Irishman and Captain Jamy the Scotsman all speak their funny English'. Peter Burke, *Hybrid Renaissance: Culture, Language, Architecture*, Natalie Zemon Davis Annual Lectures Series (Budapest: Central European University Press, 2016), p. 111.

Greenblatt's reading of the scene in, perhaps, his most influential essay about Shakespeare:

> By yoking together diverse peoples – represented in the play by the Welshman Fluellen, the Irishman Macmorris, and the Scotsman Jamy, who fight at Agincourt alongside the loyal Englishmen – Hal symbolically tames the last wild areas in the British Isles, areas that in the sixteenth century represented, far more powerfully than any New World people, the doomed outposts of a vanishing tribalism.[248]

Even Greenblatt's language of 'yoking ... diverse peoples' from 'wild areas' and the symbolic taming of representatives of 'a vanishing tribalism', seems to validate, if not justify and approve, any such suppression by Henry V or another English monarch. And 'the loyal Englishman' does not hold copyright on loyalty. Is the Welsh Captain's loyalty to his Welsh king ever in question? Other influential examples abound. In her discussion of the second tetralogy, Catherine Belsey viewed the four captains scene as a comic interlude, having first rehearsed the claim that it was an interpolated scene.[249] That the Celtic captains are viewed as comic characters within criticism is arguably at odds with how they are presented within the drama, but Belsey fixes on the perceived stereotypes:

> The characterisation of the figures representing the nations which make up the British Isles is consistent, on the whole, with the national stereotypes who were to reappear in an almost endless succession of subsequent British jokes. Captain Jamy, the Scotsman, is as dour as Fluellen is verbose; Macmorris is an irascible Irishman; and Gower, the Englishman, and the only one who displays complete

[248] Stephen J. Greenblatt, 'Invisible Bullets: Renaissance Authority and Its Subversion, Henry IV and Henry V', in Jonathan Dollimore and Alan Sinfield, eds., *Political Shakespeare: Essays in Cultural Materialism* (Manchester: Manchester University Press, 1985), p. 42 (pp. 18–47).

[249] Catherine Belsey, 'The Illusion of Empire: Elizabethan Expansionism and Shakespeare's Second Tetralogy', *Literature and History* 1, 2 (1990): 16 (13–21).

command of the English language, is (of course) calm, rational and authoritative. The comedy of figures whose power – or lack of it – is in direct proportion to their mastery of English constitute a recurrent concern of comedy in the history plays.[250]

In fact, by belittling the scene Belsey reveals something significant. She locates the violence of the play and its focus on national identity in this site of displacement:

Captain Jamy speaks a Scottish dialect that has at least a certain autonomy; Fluellen has serious trouble with his English consonants; and the Irishman is barely coherent – though perfectly intelligible, to the extent that the audience is left in no doubt that he is perpetually on the verge of violence. Macmorris's main profit from having learnt English seems to be that he knows how to curse. . . . Macmorris's only other declared interests are apparently in blowing up the town, slitting throats and cutting off Fluellen's head.[251]

These 'declared interests' of the Irish Captain come to a head for Belsey in the fact that, she believes, he comes to precisely exemplify the war crimes advocated by Henry V in a scene from which the Irish Captain is absent. Commenting on the Welsh Captain's claim that the Irish Captain 'is an undisciplined soldier and an ass', Belsey remarks:

Nothing that Macmorris himself says in the course of his brief appearance in the play does anything to contradict Fluellen's view. And when in the next scene the King threatens the citizens of Harfleur that if his soldiers get out of control, they will rape and murder and spit babies on pikes, no doubt we are invited to think of Captain Macmorris in particular.[252]

---

[250] Belsey, 'The Illusion of Empire', p. 16.
[251] Belsey, 'The Illusion of Empire', p. 17.
[252] Belsey, 'The Illusion of Empire', p. 17.

This is a bizarre statement. The Irish Captain has a specific remit for the siege warfare in which the army he is fighting for is engaged. The first we hear of him is that the Duke of Gloucester has given him the 'order of the siege', and the English Captain acclaims him as 'a very valiant gentleman'. The Welsh Captain disagrees with such praise, but, then again, the Welshman has a specific reason for this disagreeing. He thinks that breaking through the siege using the mines is (a) against the spirit of warfare and (b) bound for failure:

> To the Mynes? Tell you the Duke, it is not so good to come
> to the Mynes: for looke you, the Mynes is not according to
> the disciplines of the Warre; the con-cauities of it is not
> sufficient: for looke you, th'athuersarie, you may discusse
> vnto the Duke, looke you, is digt himselfe foure yard vnder
> the Countermines: by Cheshu, I thinke a will plowe vp all, if
> there is not better directions. (3.3.3–8)

In this context, the Irish Captain, as the director of this operation, is a vexing figure for the Welsh Captain. Indeed, the Welshman makes this explicit by repeating almost the exact same phrase about military knowledge and practice in his personal assessment of the Irishman:

> he ha's no more directions in the true disciplines of the
> Warres, looke you, of the Roman disciplines, then is
> a Puppy-dog. (3.3.15–17)

And the Welsh Captain does it again when he first addresses the Irish Captain; he makes a broader observation about what he considers proper military practice personal to the Irishman:

> Captaine *Mackmorrice*, I beseech you now, will you voutsafe
> me, looke you, a few disputations with you, as partly
> touching or concerning the disciplines of the Warre, the
> Roman Warres. . . (3.3.32–34)

As the conversation develops, the Irish Captain makes clear that he is thoroughly dismayed by how the siege has gone thus far, and how, specifically, his work in loading the mines had to stop. The key here is that warfare is shifting from romantic images of chivalry to military engineering and technology – engines of war. He is the one who encourages the other Captains to heed the sound of the trumpets and attend to the breach. Why anyone would associate the Irish Captain with the pillage, rape, and infanticide threatened in Henry's subsequent speech, is beyond textual basis.

This kind of critical slippage may seem disconnected to the editorial decision-making we have been describing. Yet editorial labour, establishing and mediating the text for modern readers, is always also work in literary criticism. The naming of characters, the focus of this study, often has profound implications for how we encounter, and therefore interpret, the text. Let us return to a non-Archipelagic example: surely, it makes a difference whether a reader encounters repeatedly the personal name of '*Shylock*' or the ethno-religious designation of '*Jew*' in reading *The Merchant of Venice*? If all the Christian characters have personal names, and Jessica and Tubal have personal names, then why the reader must ask would Antonio's antagonist be repeatedly called 'Jew'? How is he more a 'Jew', or more representatively Jewish, than the others? But, and this is the important point, the character *is* repeatedly identified as 'Jew' in the speech prefixes in Q1. So, should an editor erase that early modern documentary fact from the edition they produce for a modern reader? It is certainly a defensible move editorially in that 'Shylock' is used twice as many times as 'Jew' but any editor who manually replaces the twenty-six instances of 'Jew' as a speech prefix from their copy text must be aware of the political implications of their action, shielding Shakespeare from accusations of an embedded antisemitism within the text. And if favouring the personal name, then, should they use 'Shylock', 'Shilock', 'Shiloch', 'Shiloc', 'Shaliac', or 'Scialac'?[253] Is

---

[253] See J. W. Truron, 'The Hebrew Word "Shaliach"', *Theology* 51, 335 (1948): 166–170. Truron claims the name means 'representative'. See also Gregory Dix, 'The Christian Shaliach and the Jewish Apostle: A Reply', *Theology* 51, 337 (1948): 249–256. John Upton's *Critical observations on Shakespeare* (Dublin: George and Alexander Ewing, 1747) notes Shakespeare's anglicization: 'The

there a case for retaining 'Shylock' because it has become the culturally
ingrained form of the character's name? Does Shakespeare's anglicized
transliteration of an uncertain Jewish (or Jewish-sounding) name give an
editor, and subsequent editors, license to reproduce it ad infinitum? The
conservative view would be that, yes, we are reading Shakespeare, and
Shakespeare chose the form of the personal name, and therefore we
should accept it. But is there another?

Practices of regularization with names have long been adopted by
editors to assist the reader. Yet such practices need revisiting, or, at the
very least, much greater explanation. To be clear, we are not advocating for
un-editing the text, compelling readers to turn to original-spelling editions
or transcripts of the early printed playbook, but rather for an editorial
process that explains clearly the names selected and makes visible the
decision-making behind this. The four captains scene in *Henry V* provide
only a starting point for this critical and editorial approach. Our study
encourages readers and editors to be more fully aware of the naming of
characters in modern-spelling editions of Shakespeare's plays and other
early modern drama. There is a political imperative to such awareness:
names, and the process of naming, operate within power structures that
existed in Shakespeare's time and remain instituted in our own. Who gets to
choose what someone (some character) is named is, of course, politically
fraught, recalling historical processes of colonization, forced migration, and
cultural usurpation that have a long and hateful legacy and persist today. In
a time – our own – when pronouns have assumed a fresh significance, and
when the concept of 'deadnaming' has taken on a damaging force, how
much more do proper names matter? Shakespeare, as author, reproduces
from sources and/or selects names for his characters. All authors do. These
designations inform us about Shakespeare's vision for these characters, but
also tell us about a broader early modern cultural understanding of the
relationship between name and identity. Shakespeare was content to use

Jew's name in the *Merchant of Venice*, *Scialac*, he makes English and calls
Shylock' (p. 240). Upton prefaces this by saying: 'However our Shakespeare
does not abuse proper names like Chaucer or Spencer, tho' he has elegantly
suited many of them to the English mouth' (p. 239).

'Jew', 'Irish', and 'Moor' to identify characters in his scripts, or to introduce anglicized versions of non-Anglophone names such as 'Othello' or 'Hamlet' for English actors and audiences.[254] As we have seen, the editor, regularizing the Shakespearean text, also reproduces and/or selects designations for Shakespeare's characters. We need to ask on what basis are editors reproducing and/or selecting the names they foreground, and how does such editorial decision-making affect the Shakespearean textual product we are using, reading, teaching, and performing?

Shakespeare's actions in anglicizing and regularizing names, which extends to placenames as well as personal names, are entirely explicable if we view his plays, as we should, as a light entertainment product for a specific regional market. He was catering to audiences in London and the provinces, in terms of taste, experience, and capability.[255] His are English versions of what are, very often, non-English plots, involving non-English characters, motivated by non-English values. Regardless of period or setting, characters speak in (primarily) English, are assigned anglicized names, and live or travel to places and spaces with anglicized names. Yet the time has long since passed when Shakespeare's audiences and readership were regional. As Shakespeare has been performed and read globally, and, indeed, held up as an international, or rather transnational, exemplar of literary accomplishment, the names he chose, and the way in which these names are presented in modern editions, have entered a global vocabulary. Our study therefore has implications for scholarship beyond the Atlantic Archipelago, connecting concerns with historical identity with global approaches to Shakespeare in performance, text, and translation.[256]

---

[254] With 'Othello', we might note that Shakespeare departed from his source in assigning the character a proper name, so Shakespeare was himself working within a tradition of naming and re-naming.

[255] This changes, if only ostensibly, after his playing company receives royal patronage in 1603, but we would not expect it to affect Shakespeare's practices with names and naming.

[256] As well as being relevant for Global Shakespeare our study resonates with Regional Shakespeare. See Kevin Chovanec, 'Digitizing Regional Shakespeares: Nodes, Politics, and Patterns in Local Performance History',

It relates obviously to the representation of the foreign, the other, in Shakespeare's works, and this has implications that go well beyond the French battleground where four captains converse. But keeping one eye on the Atlantic Archipelago for now, in post-Brexit Britain, where the land border with Ireland is now a backstop with Europe, we propose a rigorous re-examination of the politics of naming, by Shakespeare and by editors, offers a way of complicating any simplistic national narrative. According to John Kerrigan, 'the current devolutionary process . . . has thrown into relief distortions in the received picture of seventeenth-century literature'.[257]

After all, editing is a form of stewardship. Established editors exert incremental authority; others are 'but stewards of their excellence' (Sonnet 94). Stewards are minor characters in the drama, but their role resonates in the period. In the King James Version of the Bible, a steward is asked: 'Giue an accompt of thy stewardship: for thou mayest bee no longer Steward' (Luke 16.1–3).[258] Editing archipelagic Shakespeare – the King James Version – means recognising that 'The time is out of ioynt' (*Hamlet* 5.186). The death of James I at the hands of his own Scottish subjects was recorded in London in 1590 in Lodowick Lloyd's *Diall of Daies* for 20th February: '*Iames Steward* king of Scotland was slaine through treason by his owne subiectes as on this day'.[259] The death of the first James I, knighted in France by Henry V (who himself had been knighted in Ireland by Richard II), conveys the complexity we see as characteristic of the drama of the period. For many early modern

Shakespeare Bulletin 39,3 (2021): 337–354; Douglas E. Green, 'Neighborhood Shakespeare: Regionality and the (Re)production of Shakespeare', *Shakespeare Bulletin* 39, 3 (2021): 433–450; Marissa Greenberg, 'Critically Regional Shakespeare', *Shakespeare Bulletin* 37, 3 (2019): 341–363; Adam Hansen, ed., *Shakespeare in the North: Place, Politics and Performance in England and Scotland* (Edinburgh: Edinburgh University Press, 2021); Niamh J. O'Leary and Jayme M. Yeo, 'Our Neighbor Shakespeare', *Shakespeare Bulletin* 39, 3 (2021): 323–335.

[257]	Kerrigan, *Archipelagic English*, p. 2.	[258]	*The Holy Bible* (London: 1611).
[259]	Lodowick Lloyd, *The first part of the diall of daies* (London: 1590), p. 61.

critics, the Stuart Succession signifies the transition of James VI of Scotland to James I as king of a newly created Britain. But the Stuart Succession happened earlier. The role of Lord High Steward of Scotland was absorbed into the crown with the accession of Robert the Steward as Robert II in 1371, and the emergence of the Stuart dynasty. The title was bestowed on the heir-apparent until 1603, after which Great Steward of Scotland was gathered under the title of Prince of Wales. The Stewarts were the 'stewards' of the Stuarts. In *Hamlet*, a play of the Scottish succession, James VI and I may be 'the false Steward, that stole his Maister's daughter' (15.167–8). A text at the time invokes 'Mary Steward Queene of Scotland'.[260]

The link between stewards, Stewarts and Stuarts in the period has gone largely unnoticed, yet Holinshed records the advent of the Stewards from Banquo's son, Fleance, who fled to Wales, where he was slain, after which his son Walter fled to Scotland, where he was named Lord Steward.[261] Holinshed also records the 'Homage done by the King of Scotlande to King Henry the sixt', styling himself 'Iames Steward'.[262]

Shakespeare's histories deploy the term 'steward' in ways that link directly to the crown. In *Richard III*, The Duke of Buckingham urges the Duke of York to restore English sovereignty:

> Not as Protector, Steward, Substitute,
> Or lowly Factor, for anothers gaine;
> But as successiuely, from Blood to Blood,
> Your Right of Birth, your Empyrie, your owne. (3.7.1132–35)

In *Richard II* the Bishop of Carlisle declares:

> And shall the figure of Gods Maiesty,
> His Captaine, steward, deputy, elect,
> Annointed, crowned, planted, many yeares

[260] Jean de Hainault, *The estate of the Church* (London: 1602), p. 564.

[261] Raphael Holinshed, *The firste laste volume of the chronicles of England, Scotlande, and Irelande* (London: 1577), pp. 246–247.

[262] Holinshed, *The firste laste volume of the chronicles*, p. 1222.

> Be iudgd by subiect and inferiour breath,
> And he himselfe not present? (4.1.117–21)

In *Henry VIII* the First Gentlemen holds the list:

> Of those that claime their Offices this day,
> By custome of the Coronation.
> The Duke of Suffolke is the first, and claimes
> To be high Steward. (4.1.15–18)

The transformation of 'steward' into 'Stewart' and the consequent play on 'steward' and the Stuart monarchy has largely gone unremarked, but Lisa Hopkins sees in *Twelfth Night* an unflattering 'reminder of their original status as stewards'.[263] Sir Toby Belch asks Malvolio:

>   Art any more then a
> Steward? Dost thou thinke because thou art vertuous,
>   there shall be no
> more Cakes and Ale? (2.3.97–99)

The link remained clear to contemporaries. In a sermon preached at Westminster on 28 April 1647, William Strong played extensively on the word 'steward' from Luke 16.1–13 with an eye to current events:

> In the words wee have three things. First, his Office and condition, he is a *Steward*. Secondly, his deposition and ejection: The same rich man who committed to him this trust; doth for his unfaithfulnesse therein cast him out. *Thou maiest be no longer Steward*. Thirdly, the Account that he must give when he goes out of his Office of all his receipts and expences, the goodnesse that he hath received, and the goods that he hath wasted.[264]

[263] Lisa Hopkins, *Drama and the Succession to the Crown, 1561–1633* (Farnham, Surrey, and Burlington: Ashgate, 2011), p. 106.

[264] William Strong, *The Trust and the Account of a Steward* (London: 1647), p. 4.

Editing archipelagic Shakespeare entails attending to the loaded nature of names and titles in the period. Patricia Parker has noted the early modern 'penchant for homophones and wordplay on names', warning that, 'Interpreters of Shakespeare … ignore them at the risk of impoverishing our apprehension of much that matters in these earlier periods'.[265] The traditional parochial Anglocentrism of editorial activity has steamrolled over early modern subtlety and nuance around questions of non-Anglophone names and naming. Present and future generations of editors of Shakespeare, globally, should aim to recuperate for readers the meaning that has been lost through sedimentary practices of regularization. Editing archipelagic Shakespeare means recovering the names that have been anglicised, modernised, or excluded from critical discussion, including the names of the neighbour nations who continue to demand a hearing at the English court.

[265] Parker, 'What's in a Name', p. 101, 144.

Cambridge Elements

Shakespeare and Text

Claire M. L. Bourne
The Pennsylvania State University

Claire M. L. Bourne is Associate Professor of English at The Pennsylvania State University. She is author of *Typographies of Performance in Early Modern England* (Oxford University Press 2020) and editor of the collection *Shakespeare / Text* (Bloomsbury 2021). She has published extensively on early modern book design and reading practices in venues such as *PBSA*, *ELR*, *Shakespeare*, and numerous edited collections. She is also co-author (with Jason Scott-Warren) of an article attributing the annotations in the Free Library of Philadelphia's copy of the Shakespeare First Folio to John Milton. She has edited Fletcher and Massinger's *The Sea Voyage* for the *Routledge Anthology of Early Modern Drama* (2020) and is working on an edition of *Henry the Sixth, Part 1* for the Arden Shakespeare, Fourth Series.

Rory Loughnane
University of Kent

Rory Loughnane is Reader in Early Modern Studies and Co-director of the Centre for Medieval and Early Modern Studies at the University of Kent. He is the author or editor of nine books and has published widely on Shakespeare and textual studies. In his role as Associate Editor of the New Oxford Shakespeare, he has edited more than ten of Shakespeare's plays, and co-authored with Gary Taylor a book-length study about the 'Canon and Chronology' of Shakespeare's works. He is a General Editor of the forthcoming

Oxford Marlowe edition, a Series Editor of Studies in Early
Modern Authorship (Routledge), a General Editor of the
CADRE database (cadredb.net), and a General Editor of The
Revels Plays series (Manchester University Press).

ABOUT THE SERIES

Cambridge Elements in Shakespeare and Text offers a platform for
original scholarship about the creation, circulation, reception,
remaking, use, performance, teaching, and translation of the
Shakespearean text across time and place. The series seeks to publish
research that challenges – and pushes beyond – the conventional
parameters of Shakespeare and textual studies.

Cambridge Elements ☰

Shakespeare and Text

Printed in the United States
by Baker & Taylor Publisher Services